An Approach to Print
a basic guide to the printing processes

by **Roy Brewer**

An Approach to Print
a basic guide to the printing processes

by **Roy Brewer**

London: Blandford Press

First published 1971
© 1971 Blandford Press Ltd,
167 High Holborn,
London, WC1V 6PH

ISBN 0 7137 0531 0

Set in Photon Times 10 on 12 pt. by Richard Clay (The Chaucer Press), Ltd,
Bungay, Suffolk
and printed in Great Britain by Fletcher & Son, Ltd, Norwich, Norfolk

To Ingrid

Acknowledgements

Acknowledgement is due to the following for their kind permission to reproduce photographs:

Academy Studios Ltd, p. 107
Bakelite Xylonite Ltd, pp. 29 (*left*), 30
Douglas Baton Photography, p. 124
Bernsen's International Press Service Ltd, *Frontispiece*
James Bertram & Sons Ltd, p. 143
The Bowater Organisation, pp. 140, 141
Cossor Electronics Ltd, p. 115
Crosfield Electronics Ltd, p. 61
Crown Copyright, The Science Museum, pp. 18, 21
Ron Forrest, p. 46
John R. Freeman & Co., pp. 94, 95
Graphicart, p. 29 (*right*)
Harrison & Sons Ltd, pp. 32, 56
Leslie Hayton Photography, p. 89
The Japanese Embassy, p. 84
W. P. Jaspert, p. 41
Kalle Aktiengesellschaft, p. 44
Koenig & Bauer Aktiengesellschaft, p. 23
Mears Caldwell Hacker Ltd, p. 21
The Monotype Corporation Ltd, pp. 85, 88, 96
Nieuwe Rotterdamse Courant, p. 123
Marshall K. McClelland, p. 17
Tony O'Malley Pictures Ltd, p. 86
Oxford University Press (from *Methods of Book Design* by Hugh Williamson), p. 31
PIRA Photographs, pp. 144, 159
The Richardson Printing Ink Co. Ltd, p. 147
Ludwig Richter, p. 15
W. R. Royle & Son Ltd, p. 75
Syndication International Ltd, pp. 24, 145
C. Tinling & Co. Ltd, p. 117
The Trustees of the British Museum, p. 16
George M. Whiley Ltd, p. 129
Wiggins Teape Ltd, p. 117

Contents

Reels of paper at the 'dry end' of a papermaking machine.

1 Printing: the changing scene

This is not, primarily, a book about the techniques of printing, though I have tried to present technical information simply and comprehensibly. Modern printing is complex, and needs to be to meet the wide and varied demands made on its resources. It would obviously be absurd to neglect the ways in which machinery, equipment, materials and techniques are changing, and the industrial background against which such changes are taking place. But I have tried also to show the various influences which have shaped the industry to its present dimensions, and those which are continuing to alter the ways in which print is made and used. What happens around and about the printer's central task − that of multiplying originals − is increasingly important. It includes social, psychological and economic pressures which are strong in their different ways, and may well affect what sort of printing we shall get in the future, and what changes will need to come if it is to be the sort we can continue to use effectively.

Less than thirty years ago it would have seemed absurd to bother about such things. Printing was still, to a great extent, the 'art and mystery' it had been for more than 400 years. The public saw only an end product. Printers worked conscientiously in their traditional ways to achieve commercially acceptable results. Today the changes, actual and potential, are too far-reaching to be ignored by those who buy and use the products of the printing press. And who doesn't? Civilised society uses print much as it uses water from a tap. Unlike water, however, print is a manufactured thing − a creation, however noble or humble, of men's minds and hands. It is also a product, bought and sold and 'consumed' like many other factory-made things. Both buyer and consumer feel it right to have a say in what is made available to them by the printing industry. In my view anybody who buys or uses print needs to know something about what he is paying for.

The printer himself, intimately involved in the job in hand, can sometimes fail to see the wood for the trees. Technical change has brought, as well as challenge, uncertainty. Popular reports of, dramatic developments in print technology have informed, but often distorted, the public's view of what printers can and cannot do with their new-found techniques. All this seems to lead to a need for some reassessments on the part of anybody who cares about print on paper. Whether I can provide such reassessments I doubt; my more modest aim is to supply some information from which intelligent deductions can be made. Such insights may have a practical use for those who pay the printer and call the tune, if only by showing that there are many tunes, some of which one printer can play better than another. The textbooks of printing are many, and a lot of them are

A general view of a printer's design office.

good. I have not tried to write a new one, and the following chapters try to answer the question 'why?' more often than 'how?'

Industrially speaking, printing is a 'special case': we do not have the same feelings about most mass-produced products as we have about our own books, our personal stationery, our daily newspaper and many of the other printed items we use in a lifetime. Subjective ideas, opinions and preferences greatly influence not only the ways in which print is bought and sold but also the machinery, equipment, materials and methods available for its production. All the same, there is nothing to be gained from ignoring the fact that printing *is* done with machinery, and I have tried to explain as simply and non-technically as possible what machinery may be used by the printer and what it does. Detail necessary to a full-scale textbook is missing, because I am more concerned with purpose than with techniques.

For example, it is correct to say that letterpress is basically a mechanical process, while offset lithography is basically a chemical one. Knowing even this amount, we may reach conclusions about a number of things which have nothing to do with whether a letterpress machine is flat-bed or rotary, or an offset machine sheet-fed or web-fed. Such elementary conclusions, and some guesswork or deduction, may lead us away from the machines, but into an area of no less importance – that which lies between the printer and his customer – and may have a lot to do with the quality of their communication. Under present-day conditions this area is often poorly mapped and full of traps for the uninformed. The increased

A selection of printed material; this picture gives some idea of the diversity of the modern printer's products.

versatility of modern production equipment and new materials, and the higher speeds and quality ranges of modern presses, have brought complexity to the structure of printing. The classic attitude of 'getting the stuff to the printer' and letting him get on with the job of producing the required number of copies is no longer sensible or even, in many cases, possible when 'the stuff' happens to be capable of reproduction by any one of a number of different processes using many different techniques and materials.

One of the most artificial bits of compartmentalisation in printing today is that between the printer, the print buyer and the user or consumer of print. The print buyer may be a professional who knows his job well enough to juggle with the technical, economic and aesthetic facets of a printing job with consummate skill; but, in wider terms, he is anybody who pays a printer to do a job. And, of course, an essential partner in the transaction is the reader, or consumer, of print. The reader may not know or care how the work was planned and produced; he may not even notice how well or badly it has been done. But he is the one who uses it and, quite rightly, he has a voice. He may, in the end, be content to say that a book he sees is 'too expensive', or that it 'hasn't got good pictures'. This is not a technical criticism, yet it is an effective one if it means that he is not prepared to buy what the publisher has offered for sale. In this respect it is he, and others like him, who are effectively 'print buyers', for they are print consumers, and print is made to be consumed – some of it quickly and unobservantly, like Bingo cards, some more slowly, like books.

My interest, therefore, is in the topography of that no-man's-land where neither printer, nor print buyer nor print consumer has the only say, but all need to reach some kind of understanding if the printing industry is to go on serving an ever-increasing number of needs as well as it has in the past. The production of an item of print is as much an exercise in communication as one of technical ability. Obviously the more we know about what printers can and cannot do the better we can decide what we want of them in a particular situation. Equally obviously, the printer himself must be responsive to current requirements or he will not find customers.

Two themes which will constantly recur throughout this book are the diversity of print and the variety within that diversity. Because there is more to choose from, more care is needed to get value from the many different kinds of print we use. The situation is further complicated for the inexperienced buyer by the fact that, to cope more profitably with today's needs, the printer may decide to specialise, either narrowly (as in the case of those who undertake only one category of work, such as security printing or packaging) or more widely, though still within particular categories, such as the printing of journals, books or long-run gravure. But limitations of plant and equipment can be over-stressed: it is surprising how flexible printing processes are within the parameters set by various methods of reproduction. Yet, increasingly, printers are finding that their concept of printing as a 'service' industry adapting to many differing requirements is having to be modified to one which regards print as a consumer product and, as such, be measured accurately to the needs of various markets. This does not mean that the buyer of print can no longer get exactly what he wants, provided he *knows* exactly what he wants and is prepared to pay for it. It does mean that he must be able to define his requirements accurately.

On my desk at the moment are details of a book which reproduces the manuscript of the Great Tournament Roll of 1511 (when a tournament was arranged to celebrate the birth of a son to Katharine of Aragon and Henry VIII) which took nearly five years to print and in which the six-colour reproductions are embellished by the printer by the application of gold leaf in place of the more usual gold or bronze inks used to replicate gold illumination. Plenty of such instances can be found to show that, within the printing industry, there are adequate resources and skills to do 'bespoke' work of this and many other kinds: but it would be unwise (and could be expensive) to assume that, because some printers can rise to such occasions, all printers can and will respond instantly to the passing whims of taste, fashion and the customer's preferences.

It is the task of defining the job, suiting the process to the job and carrying out the work so that all controllable elements combine towards an economically produced run which concerns everybody who has anything to do with the production of a piece of print. Sometimes the solution is easy – a matter, perhaps, of selecting the most pleasing (to the customer) design from a number of prepared specimens of visiting cards or wedding invitation styles. Yet, even here, there is scope for decisions similar to those which have to be made before the most elaborate or expensive book gets to the presses, should the

A page from the Gutenberg Bible printed in Mainz about 1450, the first book to be printed with movable type.

customer wish to make them. These decisions have to do with appearance, effect, suitability to purpose and visual pleasure given by the chosen design.

It would be easier for all concerned if the bounds within which a given printing plant could work most effectively and economically were capable of exact definition. The truth – as anyone who buys print widely will know – is that, in both costing the work and executing it, printers may often have factors other than those of design, utility and fixed profit margins to consider. It is, for example, possible to say with some accuracy what the most economical run for a given job on a modern high-speed web-offset press is, bearing in mind such accountable factors as paper, the time taken to prepare and produce plates and the overall cost of manning and using a big, expensive press capable of high speeds for long periods at a time. Such things may be costed with few differentials by two printers using similar equipment and machinery, since all the elements which contribute to the total cost are susceptible of measurement. But it is also true to say that, with such high-production machines, one of those printers may find it profitable, at the time, to keep the machine running rather than have it standing idle: *any* job is 'profitable' when the alternative is no work at all for a period when the machine must still be manned but is not productive.

In such a case (which might occur when a plant is running on shift work for maximum productivity, but still has machine-time left over from that used for the main, and most profitable, end of the business) the printer will accept jobs at much lower profit margins and cost accordingly. The example is given less to illustrate the apparently wild fluctuations of estimates and costs (which any experienced print buyer will know about) than to show that factors well beyond the technical limitations of a process can materially affect the cost, and therefore the appearance, of a piece of print.

It is rare to find an item of merchandise which offers more fluctuations in price than print. To take but a single example, the paperback book, which was considered to be one of the most dramatically successful examples of mass production and mass marketing in publishing, still holds its own, though its price may have increased by a thousand per cent or more since Penguin Books brought out their first sixpenny editions. The case-bound or 'hardback' book would be priced out of the market if a comparable increase had taken place. This may have something to do with the economics of publishing, or why people buy books, or what books are published at given price levels, but it also shows that cost – which, in the case of books, includes printing and production – is very much influenced by function, and, in turn, function is affected by *how* a book is designed and made. Cost cannot be separated from the whole gamut of typographical, mechanical, technical and other resources which go to decide what a piece of print will 'look' like and how it will meet the needs of those who use it. The point would not be laboured so hard if it were not common to find one of these elements being separated and discussed without regard to the others.

Into such interrelationships, such variety of purpose and product and such subjective influences on the printed image, some order must be brought, and I have chosen the most obvious solution – that of treating the different printing processes separately by describing the principles which underly them, and then endeavouring to show how these principles have been developed or modified in recent times to meet specific or general needs. The compartments are not rigid. When I refer to the 'advantages' or 'disadvantages' of a process it is merely an attempt to show that sometimes it is better to look for alternatives than to try to tackle problems which a chosen process or printer is not well fitted to solve. It is nevertheless useful to remember the example of web-offset costing which I gave earlier, and never to assume that technical factors alone are enough to clinch a printing argument and indicate the right answer to all questions.

I have avoided, so far as possible, technical terms which might be misunderstood by non-printers: printing has not only a large number of these but also a luxuriant, specialised and obscure vocabulary of its own. Today people tend to know rather more than they used to about printing, thanks to the many popular introductions available and the references which are made to the craft and industry in the newspapers and elsewhere. It should not,

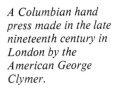

A Columbian hand press made in the late nineteenth century in London by the American George Clymer.

then, cause too much confusion if common terms such as 'rotary', 'impression', 'setting' are assumed to be explicit. Printers themselves are at variance in the use of some terms, and the correct interpretation of these can be important to an understanding of printing. I have tried to make such terms clear before using them.

For example, the word 'process' may be used, quite correctly, to describe any sequence of operations in manufacture; but in printing there is an advantage in confining it to particular *kinds* of printing rather than using it more generally to describe any production sequence. Thus we may speak of 'the letterpress process', 'the offset litho process' or the 'thermographic process', but must find another word for the 'process' which results in a galley of metal type or a bound book.

Other terms are explained in context, but it should be noted that many have alternatives, and some alternatives are inappropriate. For example, 'filmsetting' (which is in common use) does not describe *all* setting produced by photographic means – some of which may be on sensitised paper as well as on film – so accurately as does 'photo-typesetting'; and such invented terms as 'letterset' and 'dry offset' are virtually meaningless to anybody but printers and others who are already acquainted with the process. The task of tidying-up the terminology of the printer would indeed be a massive one, and is well outside the scope of this book.

The number of books on printing's many facets is large, and those mentioned at the end of this book are not necessarily the only, or even the most complete, ones: they are all books which I have myself found useful and well written and which will provide the reader with further and more detailed information on particular subjects.

It is to many writers on printing, and to many printers themselves, that my first acknowledgement must collectively be made. Printing is an industry which enjoys shop talk, and printers' shop talk is of a high quality. It has been my pleasure, as editor of *British Printer*, to hear much of it. I have learned about printing from printers, and they have shown themselves to be generous, patient and wise teachers.

My thanks are due to my friend W. P. Jaspert, the printing journalist and print consultant, for his help in reading the MS and for his many useful suggestions, to my wife, Ingrid, for transcribing a first draft which would have made many an experienced compositor turn pale, and to Miss Sandra Raphael for her experienced and professional compilation of the index.

A page from the earliest printed book in existence, a Buddhist sutra of A.D. *868. The page was cut from a wood block, the raised areas printing by impressed transfer as in the present-day letterpress process.*

2 Letterpress: the first process

The letterpress process is traditionally the basis of print. Gutenberg is said to have invented it, though it would be more accurate to say that Gutenberg was the first to use 'movable type' – cast metal characters which can be arranged, or 'composed', and which then become a printing surface from which numbers of copies can be replicated. The characteristic relief surface of the letterpress forme was antedated by unknown hundreds of years by the woodcut, which employs essentially the same printing principle as letterpress – a relief surface from which impressions can be taken, after inking, by transferred pressure, on to paper. Buddhist prayers and scriptures were being printed in China and Japan from woodcut blocks as early as A.D. 770. Even the most modern letterpress printing machine employs precisely this principle of ink transfer from a relief surface: so does the simple rubber stamp. It is this direct physical contact between the printing surface and the paper which gives letterpress its distinctive appearance – a sharp, crisp

Many materials have been used to provide a relief surface for printing. These are early Mexican cylinders made from baked clay for applying repeated designs to various surfaces by 'letterpress' transfer.

18

A Stanhope press: a fine example of the early hand press designed by the Earl of Stanhope. Such presses were standard in printing factories for many hundreds of years and many were still being used for proofing until quite recent times.

and controlled impression capable, when properly used, of extreme fidelity and consistency over long runs.

Until the development of offset and gravure Gutenberg's 'movable type' was the basis of all commercial printing. Before a text could be prepared for printing it was necessary to set type (by hand or by machine) to provide the necessary printing surface for reproduction. Today photo-mechanical methods have been developed for fabricating this essential original, and later in this chapter these are discussed in detail. Suffice it, for the moment, to say that, whatever typesetting system is used, the letterpress process demands a *relief* surface.

Early printers used hand presses, which meant that the energy required to obtain an impression was applied to the machine by hand. Later the impression, and the placing and removal of sheets of paper before and after printing, was mechanised. But it is useful to remember that, in letterpress, the modern machine is accomplishing the same series of actions – inking, positioning the paper to receive the impression, making an impression and delivering a printed sheet – as did the earliest printers; automation has speeded up the sequence and made it more precise. It will be seen, then, that letterpress, in its basic form, is essentially a mechanical operation and relies on the mechanical accuracy and efficiency of the components of forme and press, plus the skills of the operators, for good results.

The automation of the letterpress printing press is a long and complex story. It can now be said with some safety that the modern letterpress machine has reached a stage of

An automatic platen letterpress machine. The type forme is held more or less vertically and the paper automatically placed in position. The mechanism brings the platen holding the paper into contact with the forme.

engineering efficiency beyond which it is unlikely to go to any significant degree. The route which it has taken in its development from the primitive hand presses to the present-day high-speed machines has been by no means direct. Almost all important developments in the design of letterpress machines have been towards higher speeds and greater versatility to meet new demands; but a look at the products of early printers is all that is needed to show that, for quality of impression, they were often the equals of today's craftsmen and technicians with their machines and equipment.

For convenience it is worth mentioning the various types of machines used for letterpress production, bearing in mind that, though all these machines embrace the letterpress principle (that of printing from a relief surface), the ways in which this surface can be created may differ considerably. The quality of impression depends less on the machine used in its reproduction than on the nature of the printing surface – its stability, durability and dimensional accuracy. Printing machines cannot properly be understood in isolation from the methods used to create printing surfaces (which will be described later) or their speed, which affects their commercial potential to the printer.

Platen machines are the simplest type likely to be found in a modern printing factory. They print efficiently, though relatively slowly, in the smaller sizes, and are always single-colour machines. The type is held in a chase against which the paper is brought so that platen and paper meet in a more or less vertical position. The inking is mechanical, the inking rollers passing over the type-forme as the platen moves. Some simple platens are hand-fed, but most are automatically fed, the paper being placed in position and removed after the impression has been taken. The sheet size is commonly around 15 × 12 inches in Britain, or $14\frac{1}{2}$ × 22 inches in the United States.

Cylinder machines are capable of handling larger sheet sizes. They are commonly known as 'flat-bed' machines because the forme is held horizontally on a reciprocating 'bed' which moves to and fro beneath a cylinder. The cylinder carries the paper. These machines are sheet-fed, and their speed largely depends on the efficiency with which the paper is fed on to the cylinder so that the press can print a single impression for each pass of the machine bed. Owing to the large-size beds on some of these machines, the forme may be comparably large and may contain a number of pages arranged, or 'imposed', for printing in a single pass through the machine. *Perfectors* use an elaboration of the above-mentioned principle to print both sides of the sheet. Large cylinder machines will accept formes as big as 66 × 46 inches and can print (depending on the page size required) as many as 64 pages in a single pass. Many cylinder machines have several units and can print successive colours to build two, three, four or more colour images.

A single-colour letterpress machine. The type forme is on a reciprocating flat bed and the paper is fed on to a rotating cylinder.

Type and blocks assembled in pages are locked into the chase to become the letterpress forme – the printing surface traditional in letterpress printing for many hundreds of years.

Rowland Hill's original rotary printing press. The picture shows the cylinders and inking rollers. It was patented in 1835 but, though practical, its acceptance by printers was impeded by the newspaper stamp duty of that time. The authorities would not allow the stamp to be printed on the continuous paper web and this destroyed most of the speed advantage gained by the principle of continuous feeding.

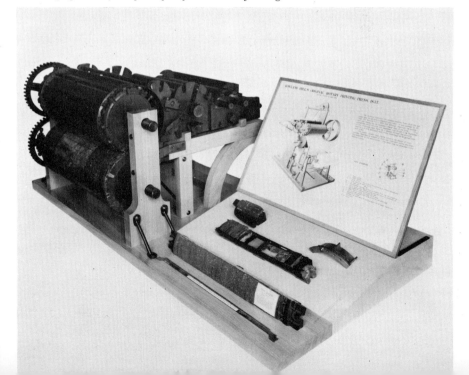

Rubber plates are moulded under heat and pressure from original metal type and, being flexible, can be mounted directly on to a base curved with the cylinder of the press. This press has two cylinders and can print 48 pages in one revolution for large-scale printing of paperbacks.

Rotary machines print from curved plates or stereos, plastic or rubber plates, or from the newer photopolymer plates. The cylinders carry the plates and rotate continuously, inking being carried out by rollers in contact with the plates. The newspaper press, printing from a curved metal stereotype, is an example of this category of machine. The paper is fed from a reel and passes in a strip (or 'web') through the machine, to be cut and folded in a variety of ways before final delivery. Speed is the big advantage of the rotary.

Sheet-fed rotaries also use the principle of a rotating plate-cylinder, but, in place of the web of paper, a pile of separate sheets is fed into the machine. The mechanical principle is similar to the cylinder machine, except that the positions of paper and printing surface are reversed, the plate being carried on the *cylinder* of a rotary press, and the forme on the *bed* of a cylinder press.

As soon as letterpress printing was established as an effective way of multiplying copies the demand for the printer's products expanded. Printing took its place in the larger social, commercial and educational structure of nations and cultures and strove to meet an ever-increasing call on its capabilities. A single example of how, throughout history, demand has called forth the development of the technical means of production is the newspaper press. In newspapers we can define with some accuracy the overall requirements of both publisher and reader. Clearly newspapers have different requirements from the printed book, which was once the main product of the printing press. The earliest newspaper with regular publication dates was the *Avisa Relation oder Zeitung* published in Germany, and by 1649 so much ephemeral print was being produced in England that it was considered necessary to pass an Act against 'unlicensed and scandalous books and pamphlets, and for better regulating of printing'.

It could not have taken long for the prime needs of newspapers to become plain: speed is first, since newspapers exist to convey information quickly to many readers. Such bookish considerations as quality of impression and durability become secondary or completely irrelevant. Also newspapers needed to be cheap: they are, perhaps, the best example to be found of 'consumer' print, used and discarded with regularity.

So, at a specific point in the history of printing, printers, press-designers and engineers were confronted with a set of problems which arose directly from the requirements of publishers and their customers. Incidentally, the importance of Britain in print through the centuries, and up to the present, is in no small measure due to the inventive genius and engineering skills which were available here after the Industrial Revolution. Many of the really valuable improvements in printing-press design stemmed from British patents, and the printing press always seemed to represent a challenge to the most ingenious and inventive of British engineers.

The newspaper letterpress machine (since we have taken it as our illustration of one way in which letterpress printing developed from book-work) is an exception to Britain's lead in the field of press design, though it was in Britain, and for a British newspaper, that the work was accomplished. On 29 November 1814 *The Times* stated: 'Our journal of this day presents to the public the practical result of the greatest improvement connected with printing since the discovery of the art itself.' The improvement was that Friedrich Koenig had revolutionised (literally!) printing by making a cylinder press which printed the whole of this issue of *The Times* at a rate of 1,100 sheets an hour. Power-driven printing presses

Koenig's cylinder machine made for printing The Times *in 1814. This was the first machine fully to utilise the rotary principle for letterpress printing and was capable of producing 1,100 sheets per hour.*

of this kind were the answer to the immense demand for more and cheaper print which has continued without diminution since.

Once the printing press was emancipated from its handcraft status and was no longer mainly concerned with book-printing, technical problems began to arise, and many of the early ones were solved quickly. Koenig's rotary (followed in 1816 by the first perfecting press – a machine which printed on both sides of the sheet before it was delivered – designed by Koenig and Bauer) sped the progress of print in the direction of newer and more diverse printing needs: higher speed, a range of different sheet sizes and, eventually, illustration and colour printing were to follow as commercial possibilities.

To remain for a little longer with our example, the cylinder press had a type forme which moved backwards and forwards under two cylinders which applied pressure and on to which sheets of paper were laid, each cylinder producing about 800 sheets an hour, the two cylinders together (as on the *Times* press) giving 1,100 an hour output. Clearly the rotary principle was, in printing, analogous to the discovery of the wheel in transport. However, the Koenig machine was still, technically, a 'flat-bed' press, though in the very same year that Koenig had pushed on to his perfecting press Edward Cowper obtained a patent for 'curved stereotype plates' which could be fixed around a cylinder and could,

Stereotype plates (stereos) being fixed to the cylinder of a newspaper rotary letterpress machine. The plates are in one piece and have been cast from moulds prepared from type-metal.

therefore, be used as a 'rotary forme'. The use of a continuously revolving printing surface in place of the reciprocating bed might seem to have been a somewhat tardy development until one remembers the associated problems.

To create the curved printing plate, or stereo, it is necessary to transform the original letterpress forme, made from movable type, into a solid piece of metal. (This was originally done by making a mould in plaster of paris, baking it and plunging it into molten type metal.) Apart from the fact that imperfections could easily develop in the moulding of a curved plate, its curve could also introduce distortion of the original due to dimensional changes caused by the curve. There was every advantage to be gained by the rotary principle in letterpress, but it required extremely accurate positioning of the paper or (as was eventually perfected in the modern letterpress rotary) the use of a continuous strip (or 'web') of paper, fed into the machine from the reel. But this, in turn, required further development of the press to handle the printed web, as well as cutting and folding it at the same rate as the high-speed printing units produced impressions so that a finished product could be produced in a single operation.

This short excursion into a particular area of printing-press development serves as an extended example of the close relationship between many different influences – social, economic, technical, practical – all of which must be taken into consideration in any observant analysis of a printing process. Not only had the engineers and press designers to evolve methods for coping with the mechanics of high-speed printing, but to do so within the existing disciplines of process and product. In recent times essentially new categories of print have emerged (such as the printing of special characters on cheques and similar documents for electronic sensing by automatic sorting equipment, or the punch cards used in automatic data processing). But, in the foreseeable future, the public demand will be for books that look like books, newspapers that look like newspapers and, generally speaking, print which is recognisable and usable for what it is: there will be little thanks for the inventor of any 'new' printing process if he cannot retain the main visual characteristics of the existing ones.

The real factors which influence the demand for particular categories of print are concerned mainly with cost. To take the newspaper again as a convenient example, nobody wants a 'different' looking newspaper, or a more expensively printed newspaper, but most of us do not object to a newspaper improved by colour. Coloured illustrations in newspapers present technical and economic problems in producing many thousands, or even millions, at high speed and low price. Colour is more expensive than black and white, requires more elaborate equipment and can fail to come up to expectations under the normal production conditions of a newspaper plant. But colour is demanded by advertisers, and by readers, and many newspapers are now cheerfully meeting the technical problems of colour runs, though how they are doing so belongs to an account of different processes – offset lithography and gravure.

The point is that while demand has risen, calling for higher press speeds and more durable printing surfaces for longer runs, better qualities and greater versatility, printing costs have had to be held down. The old cry 'penny plain and twopence coloured' implied a hundred per cent increase for colour alone! Still, for those who wish to catch the consumer's eye, be it in a magazine advertisement or on a supermarket shelf, colour, specialised design and the work of many technicians are part of marketing technique, in which print plays an important role. In letterpress printing (as in other processes) changes and improvements in quality and a demand for increased quantities of printed products have been paced by the development of more and more specialised machinery. It is this degree of specialisation which must be borne in mind in any attempt to simplify our description of the work of the printer.

With this warning we return to the basics of letterpress to find out more about its particular problems and characteristics. One possible sequence of production in commercial letterpress printing is: (*a*) typesetting; (*b*) proofing; (*c*) reading and correcting; (*d*) make-up (the assembling of the type into a metal chase called the letterpress forme); (*e*) imposing; (*f*) the positioning of the forme on the machine bed; (*g*) the printing of the forme. This sequence may alter radically in different circumstances, with different equipment and for differing printed jobs, but it shows, at its most elementary, the interrelationship of the many skills needed to reach the required result. Typesetting can be by hand or machine; the forme may contain, as well as type, illustrations in the form of line or half-tone blocks; a number of pages may be printed from a single forme of type, which means their being imposed so that, when printed, the sheets can be cut and folded in their correct sequence. All these variables influence the printer's methods.

After adjustment to production methods, many possibilities are presented by the nature of the letterpress process. Proofing can be carried beyond the galley-proof stage (when the type is still held in galleys before being made up) and proofs ('page proofs') taken from the forme itself for correction after it has been locked into the chase, or even after positioning on the press. These and other possibilities are the strength of the letterpress process, fitting it well for a number of familiar print tasks. Because it is the process with the longest history, and still represents a great deal of what the ordinary person finds familiar and interesting about printing, it retains a great deal of what is traditional in printing.

In this particular instance I use the word 'tradition' to mean more than the conventions of the craft, or the typographical conventions of the printed page. The possibility, for example, of providing an author with a galley proof, which he can alter and correct so that the changes can be made directly in the printing surface by a compositor, is a 'tradition' of book-work. The facility for making up metal slugs into paragraphs and cutting and changing the length or content of type in the forme 'on the stone' before the printing can also be called a letterpress 'tradition' without distorting the meaning of the word. The essentially mechanical basis of the process enables the printer to respond quickly, and without undue trouble and expense, to the needs of designers, authors, editors, seed-catalogue compilers, yearbook publishers and a whole range of important and profitable users of print who may understand quite a lot about other processes, but call for, and are ready to pay for, the characteristic facilities given them by traditional letterpress.

Proof-reading is an important part of printing. Here galleys (type matter which has not yet been made up into the letterpress forme) are checked with original copy by a reader. Corrections are then made to the type in the galley by compositors.

So far we have discussed letterpress in its 'pure' or basic form. The disadvantages of conventional letterpress for many printing jobs reside in its dependence, as a process, on more or less elaborate and time-consuming pre-press sequences, and the relative slowness of sheet-fed presses compared with rotary presses. The newspaper press (as has been shown) was able to secure the speed given by the one-piece plate and rotary principle quite early in its development mainly because a newspaper is, to a large degree, standard in format, length of printing run and other production requirements. The commercial printer, however, has to be able to adapt quickly to a range of different jobs in different formats on different papers and, however carefully he limits his market, he is usually confronted with the need to vary his production sequences within fairly wide limits.

An important development in letterpress in recent years has been the printing plate which can be 'wrapped around' a cylinder and printed from the curve in the same way as an offset plate or a newspaper stereotype. Letterpress has been impelled along this line by increasing competition from offset lithography which offers these advantages, together with others which are more fully explained in the chapter on that process.

The difficulty which letterpress had in taking early advantage of photography as a

One-piece wraparound plates being attached to the impression cylinder

Plastic printing plates for letterpress printing. The plates are moulded duplicates of metal type.

Matrix (flong) for casting curved stereos for rotary newspaper printing.

method for platemaking lies in its demand for a *relief* printing surface. Even the half-tone block, by which photographs are reproduced in letterpress, is an optical illusion in which raised dots (a relief surface) represent the tonal gradations of the original.

The making of duplicate letterpress plates from original formes in plastic or rubber materials is now commonplace in the printing industry for certain types of work. The use of flexible one-piece plates for rotary or flat-bed letterpress printing received an impetus when materials and methods were found capable of giving exact replication of the letterpress surface which, after moulding, had the accuracy and durability needed for long-run book-work and succeeded in producing excellent results. The rubber or plastic plate is a development, in more recently available materials, from the metal stereo already described. Apart from the facility which such flexible letterpress plates provide for rotary printing, they also have the advantage of being easily stored, because they are less cumbersome than the original metal setting, which has to be carefully 'tied up' and protected if it is to be put to further use at a later date. The forme is, in fact, a closely fitting 'jigsaw', whereas the plate is all of a piece.

The desirability of such a 'one-piece' plate is clearly explained by Peter Gibson in his book *Modern Trends in Letterpress Printing* (Studio Vista, 1966). He writes, 'It must be obvious that the precision needed by a modern industry can never be obtained from a mixed forme of movable type and illustrated matter. In the final analysis the accuracy which we require can, at present, be obtained only by making our starting point a material of uniform thickness and removing the non-printing areas, whatever the method of removal.' In discussing the different methods of making letterpress plates, therefore, we

Stripping a PVC plastic letterpress plate from its thermosetting matrix. The matrix is made from plastic and is a duplicate of metal type.

are concerned mainly with the 'method of removal' which leaves a raised printing area and, with the exception of moulded duplicate plates, all methods are subtractive ones.

The duplicate plate, however, meets only part of the problem: it provides the letterpress printer with the 'one piece' which modern speed and quality requirements call for, but still depends on the creation of an original in metal. Plastic or rubber stereos somewhat extend the possibilities of letterpress for certain types of job, but do not solve the fundamental problem of *originating* a letterpress plate from typeset matter and line and half-tone illustrations, together or separately.

One answer was found in new photopolymers developed specifically for printing letterpress. They possess the durability needed to withstand, without damage or distortion, the pressures and stresses caused by machining at high speeds over long runs. They are capable of extreme fidelity and, unlike the moulded stereo or rubber/plastic plate, are prepared photo-mechanically. That is to say the materials used for the plates are light-sensitive, and can be exposed in the same way as photographic paper is exposed to provide, after development, an image from a film original.

The commercial systems now available for the making of photo-mechanical letterpress plates all depend on a base material which supports a photo-sensitive photo-polymer layer. The surface of the plate is exposed by contact, and special equipment is then needed to fix and 'wash out' the non-printing areas to reveal a latent image. The washing out is a chemical–mechanical procedure which, in effect, dissolves and removes parts of the plate which have been exposed to light, below the level of a hardened relief surface. The plate is thin and flexible enough to be placed (or 'wrapped') around an impression cylinder on the press and be run (as the newspaper rotary press is with its cast stereos) sheet- or web-fed.

Other ways are open for the production of letterpress plates: the letterpress printer's closest ally, since the invention of photography and its uses in print, has been the photo-engraver (variously called the blockmaker, process engraver or process house). While some printing plants – notably newspapers – have their own photo-engraving departments, most commercial printers find it more convenient to use the specialised equipment and crafts of photo-engraving as an outside service. The making of letterpress blocks or plates is therefore an allied industry and is not usually integral with a commercial printing plant.

The engraved plate, for which a copper, zinc or magnesium surface is etched by chemical action to provide a relief from which a letterpress machine can print, is not itself a particularly new contribution to letterpress printing. The photo-engraved plate is used either directly, as an image-carrier, or to make duplicate plates by one or another of the platemaking methods outlined earlier in this chapter. The difference between photo-engravings supplied for colour printing and those which provide the printer with a simple engraving of a relief printing surface for single-colour reproduction are important to our present description. It is the latter which most closely resemble the original letterpress forme, except, of course, that they are in one piece, etched either flat or curved for placing around the cylinders of rotary letterpress machines.

The photo-engraved plate may contain one or more graphic elements and can combine line, tints, half-tone and type in a single plate. Photography is the first step in converting original copy into etched plates. The original may be either proofed letterpress matter or photo-typesetting in the form of film or paper positives. A light-sensitive resist, which

When a line block is made, the original (A) is photographed. If focused directly at the original, the camera will produce a negative reversed from left to right; but a prism may be used to produce a negative the same way round as the original (B). The negative is laid face down on a slab of metal, and so after exposure reproduces on it an image of the original reversed from left to right (C). This is etched until the image stands up in relief (D), and a print from the block reproduces the original (E).

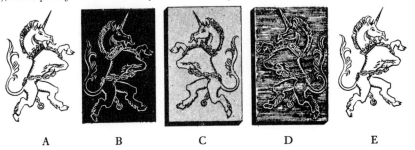

A   B   C   D   E

protects unexposed parts of the metal plate from the action of the etching fluid, enables the etchant to work only on non-image-carrying areas and remove metal by the action of the etching acid. This method of etching commonly demands further work by hand to finish the plate by making corrections and improvements which bring it to the required finish for printing. In the case of some mixed formes (blocks, line and text) the need for mechanical routing of unwanted metal can be quite extensive. The photo-engraver needs a good deal of expert judgement and knowledge to obtain good results; his materials – acids, resists and the equipment for photographing, etching, routing and finishing the printing plate – need trained handling. There was good reason, therefore, for the letterpress printer to avoid, where possible, the introduction of such additional equipment and skilled labour into his own plant, since, to be economical, a photo-engraving department must be fully employed, and most printers use its services only as and when required.

Where a printer has decided that the advantages lie with producing his printing surfaces as photo-engravings (perhaps because he wishes to use a rotary press which requires a

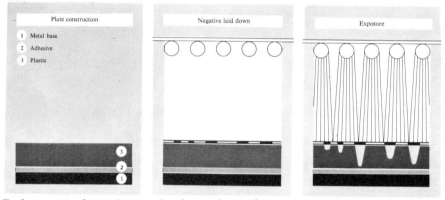

Early stages in the production of a photo-polymer plate.

printing surface etched to comply with the curve of the cylinder on the machine, or for the added precision of the one-piece plate), he may turn to some newer developments which help him to avoid the complexities of technique and economics which have made him dependent on the photo-engraver. One is the photo-polymer plate already described. Another is 'powderless etching' which was devised and came into use in printing in the 1940s and 1950s. The resists which the photo-engraver uses to coat his plates are many and various, depending mainly on the material of the plate, but all are light-sensitive and are chemically changed under intense light at the printing-down stage. The powder is required at the etching stage to maintain the correct 'profile' of the finished printing surface. The theory and practice of maintaining correct etching depths and – equally important – avoiding the effect of weakening the printing surface by etching the metal laterally – i.e. *underneath* as well as to the side of the exposed (non-etched) areas – is complex and requires special powders applied during etching to control the action of the etching medium. Powderless etching was introduced to remove these sensitive manual methods of control and provide the printer with a machine which would carry out the etching of a plate, after exposure in the process camera, as an automatic operation.

Powderless etching became widely used, not only by photo-engravers but, because of its simplicity compared with earlier methods, by printers, who now found themselves equal to the task of making their own engravings. The powderless etching machine overcomes the problem of control in etching a plate by a protective deposit incorporated in the plate itself which is released by the power of the etchant thrown against it inside the machine. The deposit, which is acid resistant, builds up in the correct amounts on the sides of the image profile, regulating the effect of the etchant on the side-walls of the image. There are a number of commercially available systems which differ in detail and in equipment required, but each is, basically, a means for replacing conventional photo-engraving with a machine which carries out the etching of plates in a single automatic operation. These

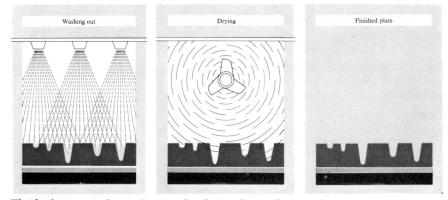

The final stages in the production of a photo-polymer plate.

machines will etch flat or curved plates in larger sizes and at higher speeds than was possible by conventional photo-engraving techniques.

Electronics have also come to the aid of the printer in many different ways, not least in letterpress blockmaking. For the letterpress printer the problem of obtaining a relief surface is paramount. We have seen how this can be done by the traditional method of typesetting for type areas, by the making of duplicate moulded plates from the original metal forme, by the making of plastic and other synthetically constructed plates by photo-mechanical methods and by conventional photo-engraving and powderless etching. All these methods are, in their different ways, capable of reproducing not only type but also the line-and-tone and photographic half-tone images which are called for in letterpress reproduction. In differing ways the printer is seeking to provide himself with the 'right' surface from which to print a particular type of job in the most efficient and economical way available – to respond technically to the varying requirements of those categories of work which he is equipped to carry out. Electronic engraving supplies yet another answer to the problem of making a relief surface other than that obtained from conventional photo-engraving.

Electronic engraving (or, more accurately, electro-mechanical engraving) replaces the 'photo' of photo-engraving with 'electro', providing a clue to its characteristics. It converts an original illustration into a printable relief image by machines, all of which have as their basis a capacity for translating a scanned image into electrical impulses and using these impulses to operate a stylus which cuts into a plastic surface to remove material and produce a half-tone 'block'. The first electronic engraving machines were introduced about 1948, and employed two cylinders rotating on a common shaft with copy on one cylinder and a sheet of plastic on the other. The copy is scanned by a 240-cycle light source, the signal from this is picked up by a photomultiplier and, in proportion to the variations of light transmitted from the tonal gradations of the original, the stylus penetrates the plastic so that the non-cut area forms the raised printing surface of the block, the rest of which is removed to differing depths by the stylus. Certain adjustments of the controls compensate for variations in the original, and it has been found that electronic engraving will provide half-tones at speed and without any of the more complicated materials and methods of control which are part of conventional engraving. Electronic engraving has proved particularly useful where letterpress printers have to use large quantities of half-tone illustrations, as they do in newspaper production.

The different methods of securing a relief image for letterpress may seem confusing and, indeed, the printer hardly ever employs all of them in a single plant. Each is suited to a purpose, and the purpose is, as always, to meet the particular needs of the job in hand. From the standpoint of the customer it is unlikely that the choice of printing surface – duplicate plate, photo-mechanical plate, electronically engraved block, etc – will be directly reflected in the overall cost of the work to any degree, since this cost includes paper, machining and, possibly, typesetting as its main elements. The techniques and equipment mentioned contribute to the greater *flexibility* of the letterpress process and, to this degree, allow buyers of print to gain whatever advantages the process offers in the final appearance of the print, or the convenience of more efficient or cheaper production in specific categories of work. Undoubtedly, for the printer, the major advantage of arriving at a letterpress printing surface via photographic or photo-mechanical means, rather than by straight hot metal composition and blockmaking by conventional photo-engraving, is that his process can more actively compete with the advantages offered by offset – mainly platemaking from scanned or photographed originals. The gain in importance of the offset process has stimulated letterpress into these important extensions of its traditional techniques and materials, though none produce a printing surface as simply, directly and cheaply as the offset plate. In all processes where the printing surface is produced as a single piece the stage at which the design of the print must be decided upon is earlier than in conventional letterpress, where the different components of the forme are physically separate and manoeuvrable, and can therefore be rearranged or altered manually up to machining. In exchange for the flexibility and speed which platemaking brings, and its economies in using illustration, the customer's decision on what he wants – how the print ought to look and how well his specifications are suited to the job in hand – must play a new part. The various methods of letterpress printing so far explained – with a few others for special purposes – alter the strategy, so to speak, of letterpress print buying.

For example, the role of papers and inks are more important when using some of the new letterpress printing techniques than they were in conventional letterpress: high-speed printing alone creates drying problems on papers where the impression lies fresh on a hardened surface (art papers) and there is greater risk of set-off or other damage to the printed image. The decision to use such papers for a particular job may in turn be a deciding factor in the way in which the plates will be made and the type of machine on which the job can be run.

Productivity and efficiency are criteria of an industrial process, and the letterpress process has had to take careful stock of its capabilities since it has been so strongly challenged by other processes after years of complete domination. It should be remembered that the letterpress principle was the *sole* preoccupation of the many inventors and improvers who guided printing from its early beginnings to an extremely advanced and automated industry. So, while letterpress reaped the benefits of a long and well-tested methodology, during which it could draw freely on the inspiration and skills of its developers, the emergence of offset as a commercial process brought not only a competitive method of printing but also an increase in the number and variety of markets in which letterpress had to hold its own.

Thus it is not only cost which influences the choice of process but also the different capabilities of offset and gravure which present the letterpress printer with new challenges: his machinery, equipment and materials must, if they are to compete, be extended and improved to cover, so far as possible, the *effects* and *styles* achieved by other processes where these are compatible, and they must remain competitive on costings.

An insight into the particular problems of productivity in letterpress printing was given by the Department of Scientific & Industrial Research's publication *Productivity in Letterpress Printing* in 1961, and the intervening years have not substantially affected its conclusions. The survey was conducted by the Printing and Allied Trades Research Association (now the Printing and Packaging Industries Research Association) and goes into considerable detail in comparing productivity in terms of 'impressions produced' by firms of different size and producing different categories of printed products. The actual running of the machines studied was estimated at only about 40 per cent of the time they were manned. The production of machines, under these conditions, is said in the survey to be about 1,000 impressions per hour and, significantly, it is suggested that, even if double the speed were achieved, production would increase by only a quarter. The reason for this is the production time lost in letterpress (and, in different degrees, by other processes)

The copper coating for wraparound letterpress plates is applied to the base in a whirler which, at speed, spreads the coating evenly over the surface of the plate.

when the machines are not running. Such 'down time' on the machines can be caused by necessary or unexpected delays in the many stages which precede the starting of the presses. Obviously the faster the presses, the greater the likelihood that their productivity will far exceed that of other parts of the plant, such as typesetting, platemaking, proofing, etc. And it is not only the printer's machinery, equipment and methods which create this imbalance: the delays inherent in dealing with authors, publishers, illustrators and others, when proofs are corrected, colours checked and many other details examined, are also part of the problem.

'Unproductive' work, is liable to be present in all printing processes: plates must be made for offset and cylinders for gravure, composition, proofing, colour separation, etc, are necessary for some jobs. With conventional letterpress, the printing forme itself can be corrected, rearranged and replaced up to, and including, the time of the actual run. It is this factor which has been both the strength and weakness of the letterpress process: strength, because it provides exactly what most customers want – a 'real' printed proof which can be shaped accurately to their latest concept of the finished work. A comparable situation to that of offset and gravure is reached when letterpress machines use plates, or stereos, which are all one piece of material and cannot be corrected after making.

The weakness of traditional letterpress is best expressed by saying that the customer (reasonably enough) is concerned only with the finished work and, while he may recognise the need for paying the printer for preparation – i.e. for the whole job, culminating in the printing of the required number of copies – he is (equally reasonably) not prepared to pay for production time lost on presses due to a lack of synchronisation in the scheduling of work and its routing through the print factory caused by extensive correction and the resulting delay in machining.

Some idea of the variety of different operations carried out on the machine alone before, during and after the work is running is noted in *Productivity in Letterpress Printing*, which lists no fewer than forty-one of these. Many are mechanical adjustments which have to be carried out every time a new forme or plate is put on the press; other on-press procedures are needed to bring the printing surface itself up to the required standard. This 'making ready' of the printing surface and press is a reminder that, though the printing machine has reached an advanced stage of automation, it is by no means *simply* an automatic machine and requires skill to use correctly. The physical properties of materials – inks and paper – are not stable or exactly predictable, and the characteristics of type formes vary. Finally, sheets must be inspected at the proofing stage *and* on the run so that identity between proofs and finished print can be maintained.

The length of run has much to do with productivity in terms of machine utilisation. If we look at the gravure process we find the preparation, production and handling of metal cylinders (the printing surface used by gravure) represent considerable time and effort preceding the actual printing. The cost of producing gravure cylinders, the time taken and the special skills involved have contributed strongly to the belief that gravure, to be economic, needs long runs: short runs of a few thousand copies will hardly ever justify the use of the gravure process. Comparably, web offset, where the machines have to be 'run up' to secure the required print quality and then run at high speeds, is also usually a long-run process. Sheet-fed machines in both the letterpress and offset litho processes are more suited to the shorter run (other factors being equal), and the economics of pre-press procedures therefore assume great significance: where machines are used for a variety of different printing jobs, each requiring similar preparation, the preparation time is multiplied and becomes a hindrance to optimum productivity.

Productivity, in any printing process, is not entirely under the printer's control. Delays in returning proofs, unwillingness on the part of the customer to accept standardisation of size or materials and other frustrations contribute to the unproductive gap between finalising the required image and printing it.

Here we are focused pretty accurately on the real problems in printing today, and on the reason for a large and varied number of new developments, all of which are aimed at simplifying, speeding up or standardising pre-press procedures. If we regard the composition of text as a 'pre-press procedure' (which, strictly speaking, it is), together with the many platemaking, blockmaking and other off-press necessities, we can agree that, whatever the process, it is what people are prepared to do and think about the material *before* it is printed which is vital to the actual business of printing it. Primarily, of course, the problems revolve around the equipment available to carry out the work efficiently and well; but there is an increasing need for those who buy and use print to measure what they want to achieve against what the printing plant can most efficiently and, therefore, economically provide.

This means the customer getting to know (or at least understanding the printer when he explains) what can and cannot be done within the limitations of a given process. It also imposes on the printer the responsibility for communicating to his customers, and potential customers, the conditions under which he is able to work best on their behalf. This may not involve the detailed explanation of 'how things work' so much as an honest assessment of what must be decided before a given item of print can reach the production stage – the press.

The letterpress printer's training, his traditions and the complex set of relationships which have developed between printers and customers have all, in their different ways, affected the acceptance and use of newer printing methods and affected their introduction into the industry as a whole. Surprisingly enough, the rational industrial reasons for more automation, less handwork, more exact printing methods and a more economical use of machinery and materials have not always struck home with either printer or customer. Where advantages have been clearly demonstrated by printers there has sometimes been a lukewarm reception by customers, who, in exchange for better results or lower costs, have been asked to vary the ways in which copy is submitted or artwork prepared. The customer may want the advantages, but is jealous of the facilities to which the older production techniques have accustomed him.

Communication, at customer level, is one of the printer's most pressing problems, and one which is likely to become even more pressing as more is demanded of his machines. The 'art and mystery' of print has given way to the technology of print – a technology which needs comprehension and communication to function as well for the buyer of print as for the creator of print.

This is encountered in its most acute form in letterpress printing. When it is said (as it often is) that letterpress is a dying process, incapable of meeting offset in flexibility and keeping its costs down, as offset can, by shortening and simplifying the route from original to printed copy, the critics are usually not conversant with the facilities which are already available to allow letterpress to compete and to continue its characteristic contribution to the printing scene. While letterpress is conceived, and used, in its traditional ways the customer pays for its traditional advantages. The future of letterpress is secured by the extent that communications improve between printer and customer to the stage at which the latter is made to realise that what he is really paying for is the mass production of his work, and that he must therefore use design in a way which can take fullest advantage of the machinery, equipment and materials available for doing so. On the printer's side, he must be prepared to offer more precise quality-grading and costing of work, and show exactly where the customer's advantages lie in using a plant which works at optimum efficiency within the capacity of its equipment to print profitably and well.

3 Lithography: from stone to metal

Offset lithography has an interesting but rather confusing history as a printing process. In its present state offset (the 'lithography' is automatically implied though, strictly speaking, inaccurate) is predominantly photo-chemical; that is to say it relies for its printing surface on a series of photographic and chemically-based principles and, for the correct operation of an offset press, on chemical balances during actual printing. These factors, compared with the essentially mechanical nature of the letterpress process, are more immediately important, in many ways, to an understanding of the status of offset as a printing process than are the technical details of its operation. I propose, then, to look briefly at this preliminary point before dealing with how offset works.

It has already been made clear that printing was, for the greater part of its history, letterpress printing: not only the machinery and equipment of a printing works but, of course, the methods and the skills taught to those who worked there were concerned with print as a *physical* entity in the form of metal, which had to be manipulated before, during and after the taking of impressions. The basic principle of letterpress – that of the transfer of impression from a relief surface – was so fundamental to printing that the offset process made unaccustomed demands on the printer's knowledge of printing surfaces as well as requiring equipment which had hitherto not been used as part of a commercial printing process. Not only this, but the offset process itself was sufficiently different from letterpress to bring about changes in the labour structure of the industry which resulted in a division of processes along trade-union lines, and brought some conflicts of interest and opinion between the master printer and his labour force. Later these internal stresses were to prove strong and, in specific instances, even destructive of the unimpeded development of offset as an additional printing process.

The technical differences between letterpress and gravure are equally basic, but, in the case of gravure, its markets are well defined and the process rarely competes directly with letterpress or offset. As a comparatively new process, offset faced several development problems. With a secure and well-understood process at his fingertips, the printer required a good deal of persuading that offset offered him, or his customers, many advantages in return for the considerable outlay in machinery, equipment, materials and skilled labour which it called for. Printers felt insecure, initially, with the optical, chemical and physical basis of offset reproduction, and with the delicate physical balances which replaced the mechanical certainties of their traditional process. The trade unions reflected this unease when they insisted on precise demarcations when offset printing started its commercial career, though many such demarcations began to look arbitrary and obstructive when the process became more automated and exact. The craft skills which offset called for in the early years of its development as a commercial printing process have been progressively replaced by a growing automation and sophistication of machines, equipment and materials.

In the event, the advantages of offset were such that the printer could not ignore them: the demands of his customers – particularly for colour printing and more illustration – together with the rising cost of expanding the scope of letterpress to take in new fields of print called for change. This demand, and other commercial factors, forced some printers to see offset as a way towards new markets and an alternative to letterpress in serving some existing ones.

The commercial success of offset was enough to create a situation which printing had never before faced in such an acute form: a choice of major processes became available. Offset printing was sold competitively in such a way that whole sectors of the letterpress printer's market were crumbled away by the new offset houses, many of which started from scratch without the preconceptions and preoccupations which any printer with a plant already dedicated, by existing machinery and equipment, to letterpress production, must have. The whole industry began to re-equip and to change shape in ways which influenced the categories of print it provided.

It has been as much the urgency of demand as any easy comparisons between the two processes which has decided the issue and placed offset printing in the wider commercial field as a modern printing process. Lithography has a long and respectable history as a means of multiplying originals. As linguists will detect, its origins are with a smoothed stone surface on to which a design may be drawn direct with a greasy crayon. If the surface is wetted the grease will repel water and the stone will be damp only in those parts which have not been touched by the crayon. If the surface is then inked with a greasy-based ink, the ink will be taken up by the image and can be transferred to paper by direct contact, the water repelling the ink from the non-image-bearing areas. This principle relies on a correct physical and chemical balance between the image on the stone, the water and the ink. Such 'direct' methods of producing lithographs were – and still are – used by artists seeking particular effects obtainable only by lithography – principally a 'soft' line and a pleasantly impressionistic effect when colours are overprinted and combined by several printings. Some commercial use was made of the process, and it was automated for machine production fairly successfully. But lithography did not start towards its present stage of development until the offset principle was introduced.

The image for off-setting is carried on the surface of a printing plate. It is (as on the stone) planographic – that is to say it is neither a relief surface, as in letterpress, nor a sunken or 'intaglio' surface, as in gravure. The stone is thus replaced by a thin metal plate, which may be made of aluminium, or other metals with the required properties of durability under the printing run. The surface of the litho plate is sensitised so that it is, in effect, similar to a photographic film, supporting a thin light-sensitive chemical surface on a base material. Litho plates may be made sensitive by coating with sensitiser inside the printing plant, or may be obtained pre-sensitised. In both cases the image to be printed is implated photographically, which means that it must already exist in the form of a *film positive or negative* which allows it to be projected optically, or contact-printed, on to the sensitised surface for chemical development, much as a photographic negative is projected on to sensitised paper in the making of an ordinary enlargement.

The advantages, to the printer, of this facility for producing a plate photographically are several: he may use different graphic elements – type, line and half-tone – to make up a plate, and can, by optically altering the degree of enlargement or reduction of the original negative, arrange images within specified formats. The disadvantage, compared with the letterpress process, is that, once a plate is made, it cannot, unlike the letterpress forme with its movable type and blocks, be changed to any significant degree. It will also be observed that, though metal type is not in itself essential to the production of offset-printed text, such type must be composed, since offset relies on an *existing* image from which an original negative can be made. In the past this meant that typesetting for text had to be carried out before a proof for the making of a photographic reproduction could be

A library of lithographic stones – the type of printing surface used before the invention of flexible metal lithographic plates.

An offset press with side-plate opened to show the system of rollers. The rollers at the top are for inking and rotate in contact to break down the ink into a film of the required thinness for transfer to the printing plate.

obtained. More recent developments have given the offset printer photo-typesetting (see Composition, Chapter 7), which provides setting in the form of a film positive or negative and is therefore capable of being used directly in the production of offset plates without the intermediate proofing and photographing of original hot-metal setting.

Once the plate is fixed to a cylinder of the offset press, an automatic inking and dampening system provides ink and water in the necessary proportions. The plate is not used, as was the lithographic stone, in direct contact with the paper. Its image is transferred – i.e. 'off set' – to a flexible, rubbery surface known as the offset blanket. The concept is easy to demonstrate if we make a mark with a ballpoint pen on paper and use our thumb to pick up, under pressure, a reverse image which can be carried and transferred by further pressure to another piece of paper. The image is, in a comparable way, 'off set' from the plate to a blanket cylinder in the press, and from blanket cylinder to paper. The sequence is traceable as follows: a right-reading film image produces a (right-reading) image on the sensitised plate; the plate transfers its image, wrong-reading, to the offset blanket, which, in turn, transfers the image, right-reading, to the paper.

This, in essence, is what offset machines are doing, whether they are using the process to print separate sheets of paper (sheet-fed) or are printing on a continuous roll of paper passing through the press (web-fed). A press may have two printing units so that a sheet is printed both sides (perfected), or successive printing units for successive colours, with a final two, three, four or more colour print.

Remaining, for the present, with the basics of the offset process, it is not necessary to reiterate the principles of offset and letterpress to see that they are different not only as processes but also in the types of equipment needed to prepare a printing surface. The principle of offset printing is not difficult to understand, but its employment, at high speeds and with consistent qualities, proved an example of rapid and successful development on the part of machinery and equipment manufacturers, and by those equally important contributors to the final result in printing, the platemakers, papermakers and inkmakers.

The letterpress process is robust compared with offset. While an offset machine is running there must be a continuous and carefully judged balance maintained between the amount of water (damping) and the amount of ink supplied to the plate. This is delicate enough to be upset even by humidity changes in the atmosphere surrounding the press. Also, we are not dealing here with 'impression' in the letterpress sense, but with the *transfer* of an image from plate to blanket and from blanket to paper – all materially flat surfaces and, consequently, more critical in their physical relationships compared with raised surfaces, which allow for a degree of compressibility. Early offset printing was easily detectable by a tendency towards softer colours and a certain deterioration into greyness from black.

The offset blanket and the paper stock itself became much more important to the printer in maintaining evenness and uniformity of transfer, and, of course, any foreign bodies or any radical change in the chemical balance between water and ink on the surface of the offset plate itself (which was found to be liable to 'scumming' or the formation of greasy surface deposits) spoiled the printing. Similarly, foreign bodies and marks on the damp surface of the blanket or the plate (paper dust is the greatest hazard) are transferred to the print as unwanted marks, mottles or flecks.

These, and other difficulties, have been largely overcome by energetic research and improved knowledge and facility on the part of machinery and materials manufacturers and offset printers, making offset, today, as reliable a process as letterpress and, except to the expert's eye, often indistinguishable from it. The process starts with a potential mechanical advantage – that of the rotary principle, which makes for higher printing speeds compared with the flat-bed principle, in which the type-bed moves horizontally, still used in many letterpress machines. To use the rotary principle a letterpress machine must, by some means, obtain a curved printing plate and, by doing so, puts itself at a disadvantage like that of offset if last-minute corrections or later revisions are demanded, since these can only be carried out *in situ* on the 'pure' letterpress forme, which is flat. The offset plate is, by its nature, flexible, and therefore easy to wrap around the plate cylinder.

In the wider sphere of print marketing the technical differences between offset and letterpress pose questions which go well beyond the principles employed by each. In certain classes of work letterpress remains the more acceptable process by virtue – rather than in spite of – its traditional basis. The whole question of proofing, and the corrections which need to be made in the finished job, is a prickly one to start with and has been discussed in the chapter on letterpress. Generations of publishers, authors and copywriters have worked together with their printers on the assumption that type, as a physical entity, is movable, changeable and storable, and the demand by the offset printer that an end be made of corrections after the work has reached camera stage can cause alarm. Again, the offset plate itself is more delicate than the letterpress forme, stereo or wrap-around plate, and is more quickly and fatally susceptible to damage and physical deterioration, both on the run and after, though it can be given a protective coating for storage.

Such arguments against offset must be modified when we see that many millions of newspapers are now printed this way. Because it is cheap and easy to make, the offset plate can quickly be replaced without much trouble. The majority of offset newspapers are weeklies; most daily papers with very long runs, frequent edition changes and a heavy

Developed offset plates must be inspected for defects before going on to the press.

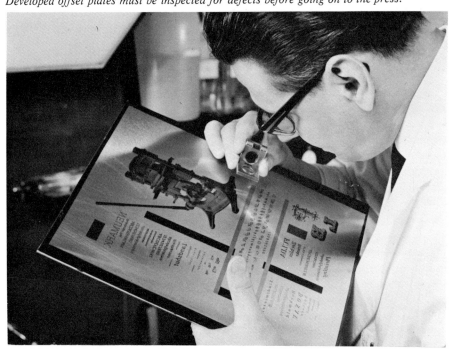

commitment to existing equipment (and existing agreements with the trade unions) stick to letterpress. For many of the weeklies it can truthfully be said that offset has provided them with life-saving advantages over their bigger brethren. Offset's greatest virtue, for them, is the comparative ease with which colour and illustration can be introduced into the printed page. A photograph required for letterpress reproduction must be produced as a half-tone block. For offset a good original is all that is needed to obtain the photographic copy required to make a plate. In some newspapers the whole production scene has been changed from one in which typesetting in metal, blockmaking, make-up 'on the stone' and stereo casting before printing was carried out for every page, to one in which type is provided by photo-composing machines (in some cases from keyboards which operate to computers which incorporate the typographical style in pre-set programmes) and the cameras. The busy scene in the composing room has been transformed to one in which quiet men with clean hands and in white coats make delicate incisions into film, fitting whole pages together in an immaculate transparent jigsaw for the platemakers.

Where the offset process is used for long runs of average quality, web-offset is commonly chosen. Web-offset captured the popular imagination in a way in which other printing processes have failed to on the technical side. Maybe people were waiting a little impatiently for printing to produce evidence of dramatic technical progress comparable with younger and less strictly industrially circumscribed industries, or maybe the public is at last getting genuinely curious about the source of all that printing. Unfortunately, the advent of web was often misrepresented, and consequently misunderstood, by many who would have found a clear exposition of the capabilities and potentials of the process interesting. It was, for example, said to be a 'new printing process', whereas offset is not new, as a process: the significant difference between web-fed and sheet-fed offset is that the former prints continuously on a moving web of paper passing through the press from a reel, and progressing to more or less complex folders, cutters and other machinery at the delivery end of the press to produce completed newspapers, journals, catalogues and similar print. It is, mechanically speaking, an advanced stage of automation which literally transforms a reel of paper into a finished product, printed both sides, in colour if required, delivered folded and stapled as needed.

The development of the web-offset machine is closely linked with the engineering and other capabilities of its designers and manufacturers, together with the research results from manufacturers of inks, paper and plates. But it is true to say that web-offset is remarkable less for its employment of the offset process for high-speed printing – a modern web-offset machine is capable of around 20,000 complete copies an hour – than for the capacity of the 'finishing' end of the press – folders, cutters, etc – which, at high printing speeds, have to handle the printed paper with fantastic efficiency and accuracy on their own account. Web-offset is a reminder of the truth that no printing job is complete until it can be sent out in the form required by its potential users, and therefore an increase in printing or setting speeds alone does not invariably guarantee higher production. Books

A newspaper page is made up on a light table from separate pieces of film containing photo-set text and photographically-produced illustration.

need binding; covers need laminating; swing tickets need punching and stringing – and so on over a vast range of printed products where the printing press does not have the last say in making the goods fit for use.

Fortunately for the publisher and printer, the newspaper, journal, paperback book, magazine and catalogue, the formats of which are roughly comparable, are long-run jobs, and therefore are at the profitable end of the print market. Consumption is high, and such items, running into many millions, also need to be cheaply produced, for they are quickly consumed, with the consumer ready and waiting for more. Web-offset was thus impelled by force of demand, and in spite of its limitations, along a successful road to advanced development.

The advantages of web-offset to the printer were not secured without certain sacrifices in flexibility and economy to which he had been accustomed by more adaptable machinery. Paper is a large item in the total cost of any printing job, and web-offset can increase the cost of the paper used by wasting it. Anyone who has watched a web of paper passing through an offset press at the rate of 2,000 feet per minute will appreciate that, in a process which requires correct ink/water balance and other exact adjustments for optimum results, a good deal of spoiled print can pass through the machine while it is being 'run up' to speed and before the desired quality is emerging at the delivery end. This 'running up' of a press to high speed may cause a paper-waste factor of 12 per cent and over, mainly at the start and end of runs. If the paper web breaks accidentally the press must be stopped and rethreaded with paper – time lost, and, again, paper waste until the press is brought up to optimum printing performance. Frequent plate changes present the same risk of wastage, since the press must be slowed, stopped and restarted for the plate-change.

Another limiting factor of most web-offset presses is that, owing to the diameter of the cylinder which carries the plate, operating in conjunction with the folder, cutter and other end-of-press features, the length (or 'cut-off') of the printed image along the web is fixed, a fact which materially affects the flexibility of the press in handling print of widely varying finished sizes. Web-offset presses have been designed so that cut-off can be varied, but, generally speaking, designers have concentrated on producing presses within the formats more commonly used for the particular print categories most likely to call for web-offset printing.

The drying of the inks on a web travelling at high speeds has also presented technical problems to press designers, inkmakers and printers. Printing inks contain a proportion of solvents which are intended to evaporate on contact with the surrounding air and, at the slower speeds of sheet-fed machines and letterpress rotaries, quick-drying inks (aided, occasionally, by special drying sprays which treat each printed sheet separately) present no great problem. A web of paper travelling through a press carries some of these evaporated solvents along above its moving surface by sheer impetus, and neither the absorbency of the paper nor the formulation of the inks will absolutely ensure complete drying, and hence no 'set off' or smudging of the printed image when passing through the press and folders by contact with the equipment itself or with adjacent sheets.

To overcome this most web-offset presses are fitted with driers which use either air or a gas flame to dry the print as it passes through on the web. The driers, in effect, 'skim' the solvents off the web before applying heat to the inked surface of the paper. The inks are formulated so as to 'set' in this momentary heat. There has been, in recent years, another form of web-drying introduced in which micro-waves are transmitted into the moving web from generators. In effect the waves 'shake up' the molecules of the ink formulation and dry the inks by ultrasonic vibration. At the time of writing these are successful at fairly high speeds but not at the maximum speeds of fast web-offset presses.

One advantage of web-offset is that, owing to the presence of efficient driers, a heavier deposit of ink can be laid down, compared with sheet-fed offset, without the risk of set-off between printed sheets, which is always present with sheet-fed machines. This allows a web-offset printer to regain some of the image quality he may lose by using cheaper papers at high speeds.

Now that offset, in all its forms, can produce print within a wide range of qualities, from the newspaper to the art reproduction, it has often been claimed that the process will eventually replace letterpress entirely. This it could conceivably do, but there are many other things which would have to happen first. For some categories of work – especially those where certain papers are used which do not accept an offset image as well as an impressed one – the advantages of letterpress remain. Facilities for early proofing and late correction have been mentioned as one of the strengths of letterpress, and in book production this is still a powerful argument in favour of the traditional process. Books which are kept in type for later editions or for 'updating' by changes or additions to an existing text reap the advantage of being capable of storage as type in page-form ready for reprinting by letterpress, though the computer may soon deprive letterpress of this advantage over offset (see Chapter 10).

In my view it is profitless to regard the offset process simply as a competitor, successful or otherwise, of letterpress. There is evidently room for two processes at this commercial level, and it would be both difficult and tedious to have to prove that offset could successfully and economically accomplish any and every printing job still being done letterpress. The printing industry is heavily committed to metal type and letterpress machinery and, in the chapter on the letterpress process, other reasons are suggested for believing that it will continue to have a place in commercial printing for a long time to come.

Of more immediate interest is the potential which the offset process has in future developments for print. It has already been responsible for a demand by printers for photo-typesetting equipment, which supplies setting in the form of film or paper positives ready for the cameras in the offset platemaking department. The ease with which it is possible to arrive at an offset plate by direct photography of originals has opened up several new possibilities for offset. Typewritten originals – especially those in which the typewriters are designed with high-quality typefaces and other facilities (see Composition: Chapter 7) – can be used in place of the composing room and its associated typesetting equipment to supply a quality of setting adequate to many commercial uses when photographed and reproduced by offset.

When we begin to look at many of the newer pre-press systems it is seen that these are very often designed primarily to be used by the offset process. The facsimile transmission of images by telephone line or radio link over distances is an important printing development, as is computer-assisted composition. In both cases the easiest way of handling the material and progressing it towards the print stage is by photographic methods such as those common in offset reproduction. It will be remembered that photo-polymer plates

A two-unit sheet-fed offset press.

have given the letterpress process the same facility with photographic plate preparation from film originals, but offset is ideally equipped to handle film or positives in the most direct and economical manner. And, of course, print which already exists, whether printed letterpress or offset originally, provides an image from which an offset plate can easily be made by photo-copying. The process is therefore of great value where printed matter is required for further reproduction, such as the facsimile reproduction of old books. The nature of the process does not (as has been shown) lend itself easily to any change in content or format (though overall enlargement or reduction of size is easy), and, of course, the updating of information requires the resetting of the original to produce a new and correct version for offset platemaking.

Some reference can be made to typewriter composition, since this has improved and become a useful facet of offset printing in recent years. The ordinary fabric-ribbon typewriter fell short of the clarity, crispness and overall typographical standard required by many customers, but modern typewriters, some of which have been deliberately designed to bring image clarity, type styles, spacing and other needs more into line with existing typographical conventions, have enabled offset printers to develop methods of using typewritten copy as an original for platemaking, eliminating the need for the considerably more elaborate and expensive methods of text composition used in the conventional composing room.

A Marinoni web-offset press.

Typewriters also provide a simple means of reproducing fairly complicated text, such as mathematics or chemical formulae, without the special difficulties which more elaborate composing equipment presents when the text does not follow the straight line of ordinary literary text. In fact, provided some simple way is available to get the text on to paper, diagrams or any symbols not available on keyboard can be drawn in. Transfer lettering, photographs – in fact, anything that can be reproduced as a good quality original – is theoretically ready for the offset platemaker's camera department.

It is a sidelight on our determination to see print as something produced by conventional methods that typewriter composition has not been more widely used. A typewriter cannot reproduce either the variety or the visual harmony and accuracy of a well-set text produced by automatic line-composing or typesetting equipment. Nevertheless, it is inexpensive and, up to a point, acceptable for many purposes where conventional composing costs would be too high to allow an item to be printed. The satirical magazine *Private Eye* is an example of the use of typewriter setting, transfer lettering and line and half-tone originals combined to provide a quite legible and pleasing result. Some printers have specialised in the production of typewriter-composed material and have been able to extend the market for it and improve the quality and range of items which can profitably and appropriately be reproduced from it.

An extension of typewriter composition is the use of tape-controlled automatic type-writers. These work at higher speeds than do manually keyboarded models, and enable the printer to use quite advanced systems of copy preparation. The original keyboarding produces a tape which controls the automatic typewriter. The use of a small, special-purpose computer between keyboard and auto allows the introduction into the final tape of a number of pre-set typographical and format requirements, such as correct spacing or indentation, changes of typeface, justification of lines, italicisation and other variations of style within the typewriter's capabilities. Copy can then be keyboarded straightforwardly, and by typographically unskilled workers, with the assurance that the final result − an original for platemaking − will follow the style laid down for the job.

A further facility which computer-controlled typewriter composition offers is that of providing 'proofs' for correction or alteration. If the keyboard-originated tape is fed into an automatic typewriter the machine produces, in effect, a 'proof'. If correction or alteration is needed a second tape can be prepared containing the corrections or new material and merged with the original tape to give a final corrected tape for the production of the finished work. This is a common procedure in most tape-controlled composing systems, and one which has special advantages in typewriter composition. A typewriter composing service is provided by some trade houses, and any printer wishing to call on this kind of composition can do so by sending his material out and receiving from the trade service an original suitable for camera and platemaking.

Typewriter composition is limited to a comparatively small range of types (though most graphic-reproduction-quality typewriters have interchangeable type) and, in common with the whole of the offset process, there is some deterioration from the original in the final print. Yet again it is a correct evaluation of all factors influencing the design and purpose of a printed item which should be the deciding factor in choosing or rejecting a method. Typewriters would be unlikely to be chosen, for example, for a long-run, good-quality book. There remain many items of print where such direct and easily handled methods of reproducing text are economical and satisfactory.

For illustrations we must look to the photographic basis of the process. Where, in multi-colour letterpress, it is necessary to separate the primary colours and to make separate half-tone blocks so that each colour may be printed in register over the preceding colour, the offset process demands separation negatives; that is the separation of suc-cessive colours for overprinting from separate plates to form the final two, three, four or more colour print. Thus the parts of an illustration which are to print red are selectively extracted and produced as a single red-printing plate, while other colours − blue, yellow, black, etc − are similarly isolated by masking techniques in the platemaking department as separate negatives, each of which will be used to make a plate, and all of which will be printed in the correct colour sequence by the separate printing units of a multi-colour press. Though offset does not use the raised dot − which is the characteristic of the letterpress block and which is obtained by screening original photographs to obtain the break-up required to print a half-tone – it is usual to screen photographs used in offset reproduction. The process can hardly handle the full range of solid tones in a photograph, and a satisfactory result can usually be obtained only by the introduction of screens, at the camera stage, which photographically break up the tonal areas of the original into a dot-pattern which, on the finished print, closely resembles that of the letterpress block.

The separation of colours may be carried out by electronic scanning, which extracts from a coloured original the required tones for printing to a pre-set range of tone-values, eliminating, in a single automatic step, the elaborate camera work of colour separation and the hand-retouching often needed afterwards.

4 Gravure: the giant

The third of the classic 'three main printing processes' is gravure. It is probably the least commonly understood. This is partly because it is, indeed, a complex process, and one in which a high degree of mechanical and operational specialisation is called for, and partly because its characteristics demand long runs to be economical. It is therefore unlikely that many of the day-to-day jobs handled in general printing plants will be printed gravure. But in terms of productivity gravure has long maintained an important place in printing, and the gravure plant is often (though not by any means always) a specialised one. The preparation of the printing surface (an engraved plate or cylinder) and the presses them- selves make gravure printing a large-scale operation, demanding of space and of highly developed technical efficiency. In both the cost of materials and the time taken to prepare a gravure cylinder the process does not compare with letterpress or offset litho. Its advan- tages lie mainly in the high-speed production of printed material with a good deal of coloured illustration. Over the length of typical gravure runs – which commonly go into many millions of impressions – the prime qualities of the process emerge: good-quality colour illustration with consistency over the longest run, the ability to print well on the less expensive papers and, in consequence, a low unit cost of print produced in large quantities. The durability of the gravure cylinder is also important in long, fast runs. One typical product of the gravure process are the coloured supplements now included in some newspapers. For this type of work gravure is pre-eminent, giving pictures and text of good quality.

In gravure, more perhaps than in any other printing process, good initial planning and costing are essential. It may, on occasion, be decided that the qualities imparted by gravure are required for shorter runs, and here it will be a question of whether the initial expense of preparing cylinders and using the big presses is justified. More commonly the gravure printer's customer will be seeking the watershed which exists in all printing processes where the economies of a long run begin to affect the unit cost of impressions to the customer's advantage. This point has not been explained fully before and, though fairly obvious, it may be underlined here.

Assuming anybody wanted a single printed impression by any process, the cost would be high, incorporating all the expense of preparing the printing surface, setting up the machine and printing this hypothetical single impression. For short-run work therefore there is clearly an advantage to the customer in any process where the required image to be printed can be transformed into a printable plate as cheaply as possible. As more and more impressions are made, the initial cost of preparing the printing surface is met by the

Testing for the precise printing tolerances required by a gravure cylinder.

rising paper cost, which looms larger in the total cost of the job. Theoretically a graph could be prepared for a job which would show that, beyond a given point, the main production cost is reduced to that of the ink and paper. I say 'theoretically', since there are so many other variables involved. The minimum economic run is virtually impossible to fix. But it is in the interests of printers by any process to estimate this theoretical minimum to their own satisfaction, and many technical developments have been made almost entirely with the aim of reducing preparation costs so that printers can more effectively compete for lower-run work.

On the other hand, where (as with gravure) the runs are high and the total cost of printing comparably large and more profitable, there is an advantage to the printer in installing quite elaborate and expensive pre-press equipment provided he has some assurance that he will receive sufficient work to profit from it. Overall, therefore, printer and customer, in their different ways, are seeking an elusive balance between what is desired in terms of quality and content and what is feasible in terms of economic production.

With gravure we have reached a point where it is the customer's responsibility to plan for a particular quality, length of run and a standard of materials which the process can best handle. Not only the character, quality and quantity required must be right for the process but, due to the large amount of material (papers, inks, etc) to be used, extremely careful and selective decisions must be taken on these and on the nature of any finishing operations which may be indicated but which cannot be carried out as part of the printing run: a fraction of a penny's difference in paper costs may not materially affect a short run, but will accumulate spectacularly over a long one.

Gravure is known as an 'intaglio' process. Intaglio is the reverse of relief, in that the image to be printed is recessed *into* a surface, as, for example, it can be in the simple lino or woodcut where the material is removed with a knife or gouge. The removal of material by hand (or by chemical engraving) leaves the alternative either to cover the surface with ink and print a reverse image of the intaglio (which is printing the *raised* part, and is therefore comparable with letterpress) or to cover the whole plate with ink, wipe away the ink from the surface leaving the intaglio filled with pigment and print the intaglio area. The latter is getting nearer to the gravure principle. The paper 'lifts' the ink from the recessed area, and it is possible, by varying the depth of the intaglio, to vary the amount of ink so transferred, under pressure. This presents a characteristic not present in letterpress or offset: the possibility of obtaining *tonal gradations* and also *continuous tone* – i.e. an image which does not have to be broken up into dots by half-tone screening as described elsewhere. Continuous-tone gravure is relatively uncommon, though it is still used for the printing of some postage stamps, and other items small in printed area.

The full name of the printing process I am at present concerned with is photogravure. It is sometimes called rotogravure, with the emphasis on the curved surface of the cylinder which makes possible rotary printing. The gravure cylinder, which is usually made of copper, is prepared (in a manner which I shall describe later) so that the ink is held in a number of cells of varying depth. When rotating the ink is removed from the surface of the cylinder by a flexible metal blade (called the 'doctor blade') before the transfer of impression. The accurate positioning of the doctor blade in relation to cylinder is essential to clear the ink completely from the surface of the cylinder (the ink is returned to the ink trough of the machine for future use) and to leave exactly the right amount of ink in the recessed (intaglio) areas of the cylinder, which, in its further travel, will transfer the ink to the surface of the stock.

Commercial gravure does not often utilise the simple continuous-tone possibilities mentioned previously. The need for constant contact between doctor blade and a large cylinder surface at high speeds makes it necessary to carry the colour in the cell-like recesses already described. Under magnification, a gravure-printed picture will be seen to be made up of colours deposited in a network of these cell-like structures. The characteristic pattern of a gravure image seen under a magnifying glass should not lead to confusion between cell patterns and the *dot* patterns made as a result of screened half-tones for letterpress or offset printing: the cells which make up the gravure screen are all of the same area, and tonal gradations are achieved by variations in the *depth* of cells which determine the quantity of ink laid down. There are exceptions which will be mentioned later.

It should now be obvious why the gravure process, at its best, is capable of much more subtle and accurate tonal gradations in colour printing than is normally expected from

Final engraving is done by hand. This painstaking work requires great patience and concentration.

letterpress or offset litho. The correct judging of cell-depth over the total area of a picture will allow for the intensification or reduction of tones in the different colours by addition or reduction of the amount of ink transferred by the rotating cylinder. The ink, of course, cannot really be made to 'change colour', but, by being applied more heavily in some parts than in others, can secure 'built-up' intensity which is not possible in letterpress or offset litho, where a consistent thickness of ink is transferred to the paper.

The gravure screen does not break up the image exactly. The ductile nature of gravure inks ensures some 'overflow' or merging, so that the screen itself carries some of the ink from the divisions between cells during transfer and 'fills in' what would otherwise be a somewhat mechanical division of the tonal areas. This is fortunate where small detail is required, and particularly necessary when text is printed. Type printed letterpress is impressed, and therefore sharply defined; type printed gravure, seen under high magnification, does not have the precise outline of impressed characters. This has not materially affected the value of gravure as a printing process: the quality of text printing is good, and the value of the process in colour reproduction is such that a diminution in the sharpness of the type profile rarely outweighs its other advantages. It would, however, be unusual for gravure to be used in an item of print requiring only text.

It is not always essential, in gravure printing, to employ variable cell depths as described above. The half-tone principle can be evoked so that, instead of being of standard size and variable depth, the gravure 'dot' varies in size, as does the letterpress

Checking a stamp printing cylinder.

dot, and is of standard depth. This is, in a sense, a simulation of the letterpress half-tone which *impresses* the dot pattern on to the paper. In colour printing by gravure tonal differences can be shown by dots of different sizes, so that the cylinder carries smaller dots for highlight areas and larger dots for the heavier tones.

The differences between the two methods of obtaining a gravure image lead into highly technical fields, but the reason for the choice between the two methods of transferring the

One of the printing units of a large multi-colour gravure press.

image is simple: cost. The preparation of the cylinder is easier and cheaper for variable-dot gravure than for conventional gravure.

If we go no further we can claim at least to understand the principle of gravure. We have, however, not considered an essential part of the process – the production of the printing surface, in this case an engraved copper or chromed-copper cylinder, and this is by far the most technically complicated side. The cylinders used for gravure are, as with all printing surfaces, the critical contribution to the final result. When one realises that 'depth' and 'shallowness' are used of cells ranging from $\frac{25}{1000}$ of a millimetre ($\frac{1}{1000}$ of an inch) to as little as one micron, or $\frac{1}{5000}$ of a millimetre (half of $\frac{1}{10}$ of $\frac{1}{1000}$ of an inch) the meticulous preparation needed for a gravure cylinder can be imagined. Gravure uses photography as a basis for cylinder preparation. The cylinders, in traditional gravure, are coated with sensitised layers of carbon tissue which, after exposure to the image, form a resist to the

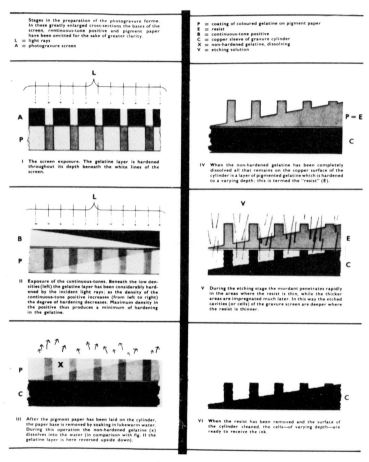

Magnified gravure surface.

solutions which will later be used to etch the cylinder and produce the cells required to hold the ink.

This pigmented paper, sensitised and with a gelatine base, is exposed under a photogravure screen, which is ruled with lines. The lines are transparent, and the gelatine layer responds by hardening (and making water-insoluble) a grid of lines, which may be 150 or

A machine used for the electronic etching of gravure cylinders.

175 to the inch. The basic structure of the gravure cylinder – its cells – is, in this way, laid down. The number of cells per square inch of cylinder varies, but can be from 15,000 to the square inch to as much as 50,000 a square inch in conventional gravure, where all cells are of the same size, but of varying depth.

The etched cylinder is normally considered the printing surface required by the process, since most gravure is printed on the web – *roto*gravure; but the surface can be a flat one – a photo plate – in sheet-fed gravure. In all cases it is necessary to screen *all* the material to be printed (unlike the letterpress and offset processes, where text is normally unscreened).

The amount of judgement, manipulation of results and retouching required in gravure exceeds that of other processes and, while newer methods of cylinder preparation have sought to eliminate this hand-work, it undoubtedly remains an essential part of most of today's gravure plants. This adds to the time taken, and to the expense of producing gravure cylinders; a reduction of both would make feasible a shorter length of run, and the process could economically be used for a variety of hitherto unsuitable jobs. In recent years gravure has been challenged, in some sectors, by web-offset, which has the advantage of high-speed production of colour work in long runs, with the added attraction of a cheaper method of preparing a printing plate. Once again the evaluation of processes must be a qualitative one: web-offset does not produce the same results as gravure and, on an extremely long run – one of millions – the offset plates will not stand up to the production of a large numbers of copies with consistent results to the same degree as will the gravure cylinder. Thus the economies of cheaper initiation are offset by the need to interrupt the web-offset run for the making of new plates.

The speed of modern gravure presses is extremely high but it is unlikely that mechanical speeds will be appreciably increased for a number of reasons, the main one being that production speeds are governed, to a large extent, by drying speeds: the print must be dry before reaching the folders if it is not to set off. The folders themselves, which carry out quite complex mechanical movements, are also a determining factor in press speeds, as they are in other web-fed processes using folders to deliver completed signatures. An increase in production speeds can be achieved (and has been in some recently designed gravure presses) by increasing the circumference of the gravure cylinder itself.

Gravure inks are, as I have already mentioned, more ductile than letterpress or offset inks, and contain a high proportion of solvents the more quickly to dry. Nevertheless, the drying stage is vital in its influence on press speeds, and the introduction of speedier drying, either by micro-wave heating or solventless inks, or by some more efficient way of removing the solvents, could enable the process to obtain appreciably higher production

Printing on transparent plastics is an important part of packaging print work. Here a gravure press is being used for plastic film printing.

speeds. The fire-hazard of the volatile gravure inks is another factor awaiting improvement.

A study of the gravure process in its various manifestations provides an interesting insight into the general conditions surrounding any printing process by isolating the steps common to all and focusing on the time and cost involved in arriving at economic runs of given quality. These steps are: (1) copy origination; (2) copy preparation; (3) the creation of a printing surface; (4) machining. Within these broad sectors, and taking papers and inks into account, can be contained most of the purely physical factors governing the economics of a particular job at a particular length of run.

5 Screen process

First the name: screen process is sometimes called 'screen printing' or, more commonly, 'silk screen', but since, in its modern commercial guise, the process uses screens made of materials other than the silk, which was originally common (nylon, cotton, linen, fibre, or copper, brass or bronze gauzes, for example), it is more accurate to agree on the term 'screen process' to describe this beautiful and increasingly versatile printing process.

Screen process is, basically, printing by squeezing colour through a stencil which is held in place by a fine-mesh screen tightly stretched over a frame, and has been called 'porous printing'. Stencilling as a means of multiplying a pattern is probably the earliest of all printing processes (unless we wish to be pedantic and insist that 'printing' requires the impression or transfer of ink from a prepared printing surface). Stencilled ornamentation was applied to artefacts and to the walls of buildings in the Egypt of the pyramids and, even earlier, in China at the time of the building of the Great Wall. In screen process, however, the stencil, held in place by the screen, makes its print when a colour medium is forced through the screen and the open parts of the stencil by a squeegee (a flexible rubber blade) on to the surface beneath.

As a simple method for printing through hand-cut stencils or blocked-out screen designs the process is crude, but its simplicity is attractive, and there will always be artists prepared to experiment with 'silk screen'. When the hand-cut stencil and hand-operated squeegee were used commercially the results were far from subtle and, at best, screen process was a cheap and effective way of making small numbers of such items as posters or banners with a small amount of lettering, where its advantage of printing large sizes (by moving the material to be printed about under the screen) and the durability of the image in the open air kept the process alive. It is rather a pity, in some ways, that the process moved so quickly from its humbler beginnings to its present versatility, for it now has many potential uses which are not fully exploited: screen process has had to live down its past! Modern automatic screen process printing machines and new materials provide a good deal of scope for skill and good taste, though they are still slow compared with the letterpress or offset machines in a present-day printing plant.

The technical differences between screen process and the other printing processes are sufficiently marked for it to be rare to find the process in the normal commercial printing house. Screen process has hived itself off from the mainstream of commercial printing, and is nowadays more likely to be found in specialised plants, mainly for packaging and advertising display, such as point-of-sale material for shops. This category of print alone is expected to produce a £70 million market in the coming years. The process is also used in

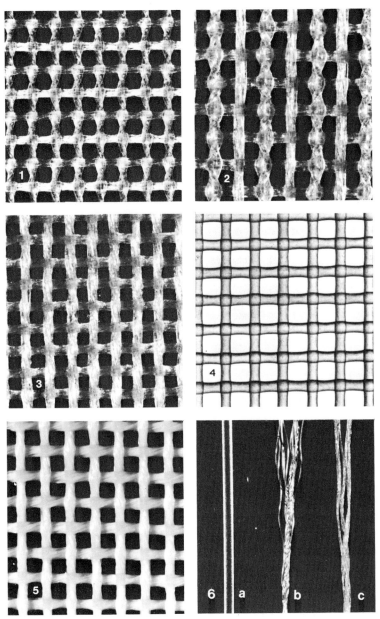

Qualities of silk and nylon which can be used in screen process.

the packaging industry for printing directly on formed surfaces, such as bottles and other containers, and for the printing of electrical circuits, so in volume alone it deserves to be known as the fourth 'classic' process of print.

The main characteristic of a screen process image is its heavy weight of colour. The colour itself may be water-colour, oil-colour or thicker pigments resembling paint, as well as the thinner inks. The printed image can therefore be made brilliant and striking, standing in some relief from the printed surface so that the print can actually be felt by running a finger lightly over it. The greatest advances in recent years have been in the production of stencils by photographic means, which allow for fine detail, and the automation of the printing equipment itself to obtain higher speeds and more consistent results. Modern automatic screen printing machines can handle between 2,000 and 4,000 printed sheets an hour; some slower automatic screens and some manually-operated machines are still in useful production.

Apart from specialised uses in packaging, the screen process printing runs tend to be shorter than those of other printing processes, and this has its advantages. Stencils of some complexity can be produced very cheaply compared with a letterpress forme, an offset plate or a gravure cylinder, so that short-run print incorporating type and illustration in colour can be made cheaply and on a variety of materials which the main printing processes may not be able to handle well or at all. (For example, a great deal of screen process printing is done on plastic surfaces to which normally formulated printing inks would not adhere satisfactorily and on curved or shaped surfaces which would not pass through a printing press.)

The heart of modern screen process is the photographic stencil. There are two methods of making a stencil photographically, one in which the screen itself is coated with a light-sensitive material which, when treated photographically, provides a stencil integral with the screen, and the other in which a paper called carbon tissue (as used in the making of gravure cylinders) is supported on a film base, exposed, photographically processed and applied to the screen, so that when the film base is peeled away the stencil remains in position on the underside of the screen.

The perfection of the photographic stencil meant overcoming many problems, including the development of special sensitising agents and film bases. The principle can, however, be grasped easily if one imagines an ordinary photographic negative exhibiting the characteristic light and dark areas corresponding with a reversal of the tones in the object photographed. Assume that the light areas of the negative (the dark areas of the positive) can be removed, the result is no longer a negative image, but a true stencil. In screen process the light areas of the photographically developed image are 'washed out', literally, by the action of water on the exposed tissue, the remaining areas of tone being toughened by chemical action to resist such removal by washing. The resulting stencil, supported by the screen, therefore replicates what has been photographed – subjects which can range from artwork in line and tone to type which has been typeset, proofed and photographed or, more usually, hand-lettering or lettering created by one of the lettering transfer systems such as Letraset.

Photographic stencil materials are now available giving the screen printer a wide range of controls over the quality of his finished stencil, and he can move with freedom away from the bold designs and crude lettering which the hand-cut stencil enforced, into the more interesting and flexible area of type and illustration. Quite small point sizes of type

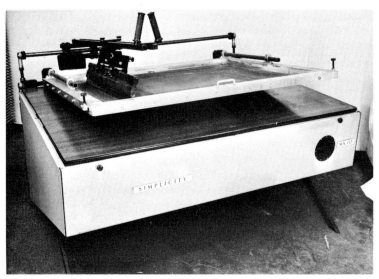

The 'Simplicity' Screen Printing Unit incorporating a vacuum base and one-arm squeegee attachment.

reproduce satisfactorily, and even the photographic half-tone is possible. With the half-tone, however, some subjects will not print satisfactorily by screen process; the half-tone itself is made up of dots (see 'Illustration and reproduction', page 111) and has to print through a screen. The dots which make up the half-tone and the mesh of the screen can interfere with one another and produce unwelcome moiré effects, and further distortion of the half-tone dot can be caused by the pressure of the squeegee.

The pigments and their vehicles used in screen process are many and varied, so that the process can be fitted to a variety of uses and surfaces. Heavier quantities of colour than those normally deposited by the printing press are often used. Oil colours exploit the characteristic richness which the process can impart to large solid areas of colour. There are many considerations which may affect the choice of a colour medium, such as whether the work is likely to be exposed to the weather, the need or otherwise for colours to be permanent under long exposure to light, special effects, such as fluorescent colours or

metallic finishes, and so on. The screen printer has many opportunities for experimenta-
tion, but must take into consideration, when using automatic printing equipment, that the
stencil must remain open and not be clogged after a few printings by unsuitable colour
media. Thin-film inks specially formulated for the screen printer can be used with effect on
many surfaces, and plastic-based colours are capable of printing on surfaces where other
processes could not give the close bond needed between print and object. Thus screen-
printed handbags, slippers and china are not at all uncommon.

This brings us to an important – indeed unique – advantage which screen process has
over other printing processes: it can be adapted to print on a contoured or three-
dimensional surface, such as plastic bottles or glass jars. Because the screen can be made
to follow such shapes and held in close contact with the surface to be printed, the process

The KPX Automatic Screen Printing Machine, powered by compressed air.

has found applications in packaging, and specialised machinery has been designed to
exploit the convenience of printing directly on pre-formed objects, such as cosmetics
containers, beer bottles and other more complicated shapes than these. This, however, is a
book about printing as it is more generally understood, and the versatility of screen process in these specialised directions is outside its scope. Treated as a printing process and
taking its place alongside the more familiar 'three main processes', it has characteristics

which will continue to earn it a place for the many beautiful effects it can achieve. It has certain disadvantages for the general printer who is already committed, by plant and markets, to letterpress and/or offset printing, and these are worth investigating briefly for the indications they give of the jobs which screen process will do most effectively.

Because screen process can print on 'difficult' materials – plastics, heavy board, metal, etc – it is often only the first (i.e. printing) part of a much longer, and sometimes complicated, operation. The folding, cutting, creasing, strutting, stringing and innumerable other print-finishing techniques which transform print into showcards, three-dimensional displays, swing tickets and other items designed for particular uses should, if production is to be maintained economically and smoothly, be carried out, so far as possible, in or near the factory where the print is produced. Where printers are engaged mainly in the production of flat sheets (and even where finishing operations include the normal equipment of the commercial printer's bindery) they rarely find it economic to install additional highly specialised machinery to automate the hand-work which must usually be done to complete screen-process-printed jobs. Of course, the printer has at his disposal trade finishing houses to which such specialised work may be sent, after printing, for the additional work to be done, but this adds to the cost of the total job.

Of more importance to the general printer is the amount of space which screen process takes up and its relatively low productivity in terms of sheets per hour. Drying was, and to a great extent remains, the biggest problem in screen process printing. The quick-drying inks, solvents and sprays used by the other printing processes for rapid drying are not all available in screen process, since the colour has to pass through a screen mesh and must not be allowed to dry immediately, otherwise it would clog the mesh and make continuous printing impossible. The weight of colour which gives the process its character also presents a drying problem when the colour lies freshly on the finished print: it will smear easily, and, if brought into contact by piling, will set off on to neighbouring sheets.

The Aerojet Jet Air Dryer, Series HC (2-stage), with controlled hot or cold air operation, automatic safety controls, self-centring conveyor tapes, variable conveyor speeds and adjustable stacking unit.

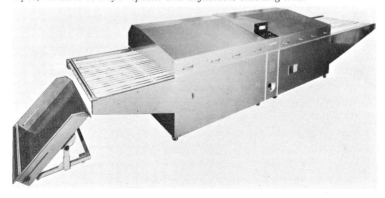

A typical drying rack composed of 50 metal trays of wire mesh,
spring-loaded for ease in either raising or lowering.

Traditionally screen process printed sheets are allowed to dry naturally, either by being
hung up to dry or placed in drying racks of various designs, all of which allow the sheets
to dry out of contact one with another. The more speedy method of drying is by feeding
the printed sheets into some kind of drying machine, such as an air tunnel which blows
warm air on to the surface of each. It is risky to remark on any technical shortcoming
these days when, almost weekly, ingenuity and invention overcome one after another
printing problem. Nevertheless, it seems that the heat-drying of screen process print can
dim the surface glamour of the image, adversely affecting one of the process's greatest
assets on the quality side. No doubt ink formulations will be found which allow the screen
printer to air- or heat-dry his work speedily without detriment to its surface sheen. The

problem of space, though, is by no means solved by the automatic driers, which themselves take up a good deal of room.

Screen process – perhaps due to its many specialised applications – is a somewhat neglected process or (to put it differently) inclined to be underestimated by the printing industry, owing, maybe, to that industry's natural preference for the high-production presses at its disposal in the main printing processes. There would appear to be some argument in favour of using screen process in association with other printing processes for special effects. One interesting example of this kind of co-operation between processes is provided by a printer who solved the problem of titling a book jacket in different languages by printing the main design (a photograph) offset, and using screen process for the relatively short-run overprinting of titles in the different languages. Thus he obtained the economy of the long run in four-colour offset, plus the economy of screen process for shorter runs and, as a bonus, the striking quality of screen process printing for the lettering.

6 Other printing processes

In dealing with 'other processes' under a separate heading we are acknowledging the status of the three main processes of printing – letterpress, offset lithography and gravure. But we should not fall into the error of thinking that the 'other' processes are unimportant. Some – thermography, for example – are indeed relatively small in output or of limited uses, others (including screen process, which has a chapter to itself) represent considerable quantities of print in special categories.

Flexography

Flexography, for example, is, in terms of actual output, an important printing process, and here we can also recognise the potential which exists in any process, namely that of developing into a more widely used and versatile process through technical development, as did offset lithography from a less commercially successful ancestor, the lithographic stone. Flexography provides an interesting demonstration of the ability of a printing process to undergo adaptations of basic principles resulting in more specialised methods and machines.

The letterpress printing surface is rigid; that is to say, in both its original form as movable type and blocks and in its later developments as one-piece plates of metal, thermoplastic or photo-polymer, the material of which it is made is hard. This is necessary to secure the printing of precise detail which it commonly calls for, and to resist deterioration of the printing surface under the mechanical stresses of long runs. This dimensional stability is also essential for multi-colour printing, where two or more plates must be printed in close register by different printing units of the machine. There are, however, large categories of print where such precision is not required and where the image to be transferred is sufficiently bold, simple and uncomplicated to allow for cheaper, more easily produced plates. These may be the flexible plates used in flexography, which, in principle, is the same as the letterpress process, in that it uses a relief surface from which to transfer the printed image. The plate, in this case, is of moulded flexible rubber which can be produced as a duplicate from relief printing surfaces already in existence. The flexibility of the plate makes it possible for it to conform easily to the curve of the cylinder, and such plates can literally be stuck on to a printing cylinder for rotary web-fed production.

Flexography was once called 'aniline printing' which referred to the inks used for the process. These were (and sometimes still are) based on aniline dyes used as colourants, which give intense and brilliant colours and are more ductile than the thicker inks used in letterpress and offset lithographic printing. The aniline inks are, however, notoriously unreliable, many of the colours being fugitive. This did not matter much when flexographic printing was confined mainly to simple bags, cartons, beer-mats and other single- or, at most, two-colour items with a limited graphic content and a short useful life.

In practice, however, there seemed no reason why, with more precise methods of moulding, the flexographic principle could not be adapted to a wider range of work. A book page is a single-colour job and, given durability, the advantages of the truly flexible plate seemed to offer the printer yet another printing process with the virtues of easy, low-cost one-piece plates. As things turned out, it was either the ingrained preference of letterpress printers for the rigid plate or the availability of photo-polymers which would provide more precise and durable printing surfaces without the need to make duplicate plates that prevented a particularly enthusiastic acceptance of the rubber stereo in letter-press, and flexography was able to retain and develop its preparation and processing techniques with an eye on its own markets.

Here a glass matrix has been made of metal type and used to mould a flexible plate, such as that used in flexographic printing.

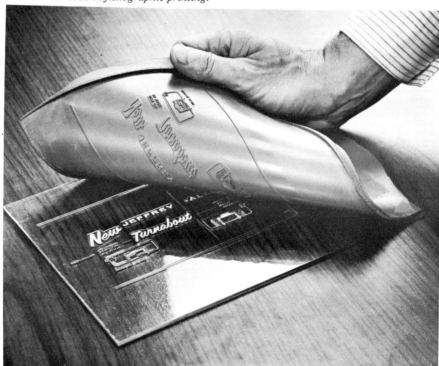

These are mainly in the packaging field, and here, as with other processes, customers' demands have expanded the scope of flexography into better qualities and a more sophisticated graphic approach. Flexography is sometimes rather scornfully regarded by other branches of the printing industry as a 'rubber stamp' process, which, in fact, is what it is. Nevertheless, even with their simplified construction, compared with letterpress machines, flexographic presses are capable of some subtlety and, of course, of high speeds due to the use of the rotary web-fed principle. They will also handle inks which print easily on plastic film as well as on paper stock. The flexographic press is often but one part of a production sequence which brings the inline principle into packaging, allowing for the production of, say, a printed plastic stocking wrapper in a continuous printing-and-making operation.

Indirect relief

The development of the mechanical principles of a printing process to special needs is again demonstrated by indirect relief printing. Here some letterpress and some offset principles are combined. The plate used is a relief plate, as in letterpress, but the image is transferred to the paper by an offset blanket. Indirect relief printing is new enough not to have settled down with a proper name yet. It is often called 'letterset', a rather ugly combination of the words 'letterpress' and 'offset'. Again, it has been called 'dry offset', which, to the printer, seems logical (since the indirect relief process does not require the plate-damping system essential to offset lithography); but, again, the term is not a good one, because it concentrates on only one aspect of indirect relief printing, and says nothing about the principle employed in image transfer. (It could also be argued that, since most people would not know what 'wet' offset was, they are equally unlikely to be enlightened by the term 'dry' offset.) 'Indirect relief' is a sound term, as is 'indirect letterpress', both conveying the nature of the printing plate – letterpress – and the method of transfer – indirect.

Letterpress and gravure are both 'direct', in that they transfer the image by contact between the image carrier and the stock. If a relief surface is used to transfer its image on to a blanket which, in turn, transfers the image on to the stock, the blanket is intermediate. The offset litho process is itself, strictly speaking, 'indirect', since the actual image carrier – the offset plate – uses the offset blanket as an intermediate image carrier between the plate and the paper, but this is a point which need not trouble us unduly. It is as well, however, to remember that the blanket is necessary in offset lithography because of the ink/water balance which must exist on the plate if it is successfully to transfer the image to paper. The flat lithographic stone does not use a blanket intermediary (and is therefore truly 'direct') but, in a modern commercial printing press working at mechanical speeds, the blanket is essential.

For indirect relief the offset plate is replaced by a letterpress plate, inked by the machine in the normal letterpress fashion. Because of this no problems of damping, as on the offset plate, where the ink/water balance is critical, arise and no ink/water balance is required on the plate surface.

The advantages of the indirect system of image-transfer are those of the offset lithographic process itself: speed, gained by utilising the rotary principle, and the availability of a one-piece plate. The greater durability of the relief plate also allows for longer runs than are considered desirable with an ordinary offset plate. The plate must, of course, be one-piece and be capable of being 'wrapped around' a cylinder, or of being otherwise made to conform to the curve of the plate-carrying cylinder of the press. All experiments in indirect relief printing to date have been carried out on conventional offset presses, the plate cylinders of which have been adapted by undercutting so that they can carry the thicker letterpress plates in place of the planographic offset ones. Some machines easily allow this; others are designed in a way which makes the required undercutting impossible.

The development of letterpress plates which can be made in a single piece (plastic, rubber and photo-polymer plates, for example) made indirect relief printing feasible, and the further development of some photo-polymer plates so that their thickness does not greatly exceed that of the normal offset plate has enhanced the interest shown in indirect relief printing. It is my own impression, however, that the main advantage weighed by printers who have shown an interest in this process is the absence of the need for a damping system and, consequently, the removal of an aspect of offset lithography which, for all its efficiency as a process, is still dependent on the machine-minder's judgement for maximum efficiency. (It would seem curious to anyone other than a printer that a process capable of such good and consistent work, and utilising equipment of extreme precision for the preparation of the image carrier, should rely on the relatively risky maintenance of an ink and water balance at the final stage of printing the copies!)

Nevertheless, to date, indirect relief printing has not caught on to the extent to which many predicted it would when it was shown to be feasible: the industry has had a good deal of new pre-press and on-press development in the classic printing processes to contend with in recent years – more than ever before in its history – and it may be that printers need a respite from novelty (to say nothing of a halt to the expense involved in installing equipment for plate-production other than that which they already have). Deeper than this lie the technical differences between the approach of the letterpress printer, which is essentially mechanical, and the offset printer, which is essentially photo-chemical. The combination (more apparent than real) of two printing processes in indirect relief printing could well be a contributory reason for caution. Some manufacturers, however, recognise the value of this merging of processes by providing their machines with a straightforward cylinder interchange which allows for an offset plate cylinder or a letterpress plate cylinder to be installed allowing the printer to choose either conventional offset or indirect relief whichever process he decides to use.

Under the heading of 'other processes', for convenience, must come a number of different ways of obtaining printed impressions, all of which are used for more or less specialised purposes. It is, however, important not to consider these out of the wider context provided by the three main printing processes, if only because they are often used in conjunction with the main processes; also these 'other processes' have survived because they possess an individuality which distinguishes them from the more widely used printing methods. Some – for example, thermography – are used to enhance the surface glamour of the image; others, such as screen process, are specialised in that they allow the printer to offer qualities and graphic possibilities not easily obtainable by the main processes. There are also categories of printing which, by their nature and purposes, require special processing, such as, for example, certain kinds of security printing (bank-notes and bonds)

An engraver at W. R. Royle & Son, Ltd finishing the modelled embossing die for a Royal Menu cover.

printed by offset but which call for the further printing of special characters for use in magnetic sensing equipment for automatic sorting (for example, cheques).

Embossing

Embossing can hardly be called a printing process in the true sense, since ink is not applied and the 'impression' is, literally, a pressing of the image into the paper surface, the sharpness of the resulting relief being the only aid to legibility. Obviously paper so processed must be substantial and of good quality, so one finds embossing, in its true form, carried out only on good-quality papers or light board; soft papers will not allow the embossed image to stand out sharply and crisply from the surface of the paper, and thin papers risk being perforated by the pressure of the embossing die. The process is more usually used in combination with other processes, so that the embossed image becomes an element in a printed design, as is often seen in the more luxurious commercial and professional stationery and business cards. The principle is simple: the image is carried recessed into a flat plate or a roller. The plate or roller may be given its intaglio image either by hand-engraving or by etching. The embossing is done by pressing the intaglio into a plate which forms a 'counter' which will force the paper into the shape required. The counter is soft originally, but is later hardened, and forms an exact 'male/female' pair. The embossing press for notepaper and the like is likely to be flat, and the process is carried out as a separate one from whatever printing is present on the sheet. The roller method is more likely to be used when imparting overall embossed impressions on to paper, such as artificial 'pebbling' or 'linen' effects, which have little to do with printing and are used mainly in the production of special papers.

Embossed visiting cards and notepaper are nowadays less fashionable than they were, partly, no doubt, due to the improvement in quality of design and printing by letterpress and offset at a commercial level, both of which will secure pleasing results without the expense of the heavy paper, costly materials and handwork required for high-quality embossing. Embossing is best used for simple devices rather than words which need to be read easily and quickly, and is nowadays more often encountered in conjunction with other processes.

Thermography

Thermographic printing is sometimes mistakenly called 'embossed'. The image, in this case, is not impressed into the paper but built up on its surface to provide a shallow relief. Again the process is one which has more glamour than utility, but is no less valuable for this. Apart from standing in relief, the thermographic image can possess a brilliance of colour and a sheen which is attractively luxurious to the eye, and even to the touch. The thermographed image is, initially, simply a letterpress image. While the ink is still wet the impression is covered with a resinous powder which, under heat, melts and fuses with the underlying image. The sequence, therefore, must be printing followed by powdering, followed by heating to form the bond. The powder can be unpigmented, which means that it will assume the colour of the underlying ink after fusion, or, especially where silver or gold is wanted, can carry its own pigmentation. If thermographic powder is shaken over a freshly printed image and the sheet warmed in front of a fire the process can be demonstrated at its simplest. Thermographic equipment used for batch production is an automation of the above procedure in which thermographic powders are applied and heated on a moving belt.

Thermography must obviously be a slower process than letterpress printing, and its glamour must be paid for. That we may find so many examples of thermographed print is evidence of the preparedness of many customers to pay for the 'luxury look' and the aesthetic pleasure it provides. Indeed, thermography has recently come of age with automatic machines capable of making 5,000 impressions an hour and solving the problem of handling a fine powder as part of a printing process by ingenious extraction devices returning the powder to the hopper for re-use. What was once encountered only in the chaste context of solicitors' letterheadings as a black thermographed script has now burgeoned into a variety of pleasingly designed and colourful letterheadings and other prestige printing, an assertion that printing is still capable of *joie-de-vivre* as well as hard work!

Collotype

Of all the lesser-known printing processes, collotype is the most mysterious, intriguing and, at its best, faithful to its originals. In skilled hands collotype is capable of the closest facsimile possible in a printing process and demands a high standard of craftsmanship. Like offset lithography, it is a planographic process based on a photographic image, but its most important attribute is that of being able to print *continuous tone*, i.e. to show tonal gradations without breaking up the image by screening. In letterpress, offset lithography and even in so-called 'continuous-tone' gravure the parts of an image have to be manipulated in some way, which under magnification shows us that they are broken and do not lie as continuous tones on the paper.

Collotype is the oldest photo-mechanical printing method. The printing surface is created by coating a glass or metal sheet with bichromated gelatine which is chemically sensitive to light. In the few collotype plants I have seen the exact formulae for these coatings is regarded as a trade secret and, in any case, the chemical and physical reactions which take place during plate processing and printing would be hard to describe. We may therefore accept the collotype plate as a flat surface covered evenly with sensitised gelatine and exposed to continuous tone (i.e. unscreened) negatives. The carbon-arc lamps used by process engravers can be used for exposing the image, but I have seen collotype plates being exposed to contact negatives by ordinary daylight, where exposure times may be quite lengthy.

The exposure to light causes a chemical change in the plate which hardens it selectively, corresponding to the density of the various tones in the original: the less light which reaches the plate, the softer is the underlying gelatine. The plate is then flooded with a glycerine-based solution which causes it to swell, the image taking up more glycerine and water in the softer areas than in the harder. When inked, the areas which have taken up the least amount of moisture will attract the largest deposit of ink. The more swollen, moisture-bearing areas, which replicate the lighter tones, take up less ink, and the final result is an ink-bearing plate covering the whole of the tonal gradations of the original. The plate must retain its delicate moisture balances throughout the printing run, and the atmospheric conditions during printing are more critical than for other processes.

Having described, as best I can, the principles of collotype, I am aware that the reader may wonder how it ever works in practice and, indeed, I have wondered the same thing myself. I can only say that it does work because I have seen it, and the results, in the hands of skilled craftsmen, are extraordinarily faithful. Collotype is used at the two opposite ends of the quality scale, for fine art reproduction and facsimile work, where no detail can be sacrificed, and for quite ordinary colour printing of cheap posters or picture postcards.

7 Composition: from keyboard to printed text

A book written in Latin and translated into English in 1659 describes the work of the compositor as follows: 'The printer hath copper letters in a great number put into boxes. The compositor taketh them out one by one and, according to the copy, which he hath fastened before him in a Visoram, composeth words in a composing stick till a line be made. He putteth these in a Galley till a page be made, and these again in a Forme and he locketh them up in iron chases with coynes lest they should drop out, and putteth them under the press.' It is safe to say that this description (with the exception that the type would not be made of copper) is precisely applicable to the work in the composing rooms of printers for hundreds of years and can still be seen, in its essentials, in many printing works today. The industry still finds it economically worthwhile to use a certain amount of hand setting and, of course, even automatic typesetting machinery and photo-typesetting is designed for the composition of type in lines, just as the compositor does by hand from typecases.

Metal type was the key to the invention of printing, and its assembly into the printed page was the first and only step which a printer could take, until recently, towards obtaining a surface from which impressions can be taken. Printing from movable type started around 1440. Since typefounding has no place in this account of printing (and is, of course, not strictly a 'printing' matter), we may dispense with an account of how type comes into being and start with the type itself – a vast range of metal characters of many designs, in many sizes and for almost all the written languages of the world, including most of those which use scripts other than roman. Initially we may concentrate on a single process – letterpress – because metal type in the forme was once the only printing surface available to that process.

An historical view of printing would have to take into account a period in which neither the methods of type casting, nor typesetting changed. But type has continuously consolidated and extended the domain of the printed word. The most important change came with automatic composing machinery, which had a difficult birth into an industry already well established in its methods and markets. In *The Composition of Reading Matter* (Wace, 1965), James Moran writes, 'The search for a practical machine which would really dispense with the hand compositor was long and costly. There were some two hundred inventions over a period of a hundred years. Many of them never became commercial propositions. . . . New composing machines appeared with regularity from the middle of the nineteenth century.' The story of these machines, their inventors, their successes and failures is a fascinating episode of industrial history and a sidelight on the

Hand composition is still a part of the preparation for printing in many plants. Here the compositor stands at the frame, his type cases (upper for capitals and lower for 'lower case' or minuscules) before him. Typescale in hand he creates a metal printing surface from 'raw' copy.

time it used to take for new machinery and methods to earn acceptance by the printing industry. Of all the ingenious gadgets brought to the printer's attention for composing metal characters automatically, only three major systems have survived to cope with today's needs for hot metal setting by machine. These are commonly recognised by the name of their manufacturers, the Monotype machine, made by The Monotype Corporation, the Linotype made by Linotype & Machinery Ltd and the Intertype made by Harris-Intertype Ltd. All are world-wide organisations, and all have strong American associations.

The Linotype machine stores its type characters in a large number of single matrices in the 'magazine' of the machine. The keyboard operator releases these by touching the keys and brings the composed characters into a position where they come into contact with the type metal in a mould which casts the type as a complete line (or 'slug'). After casting the mechanism returns the matrices to their correct places in the magazine for re-use. The type is keyboarded and cast on one machine in a single automated sequence. The slugs are easily handled and can be galley-proofed immediately a piece of setting is completed. The Linotype machines can set in a great variety of typefaces ranging from $4\frac{3}{4}$ to 48 point (up to 60 point in some condensed faces). The most modern version of the Linotype machine, the Elektron, is substantially the same mechanical arrangement for producing the slugs, but uses a separate keyboard which generates a perforated paper tape which, input to the machine, allows it to operate at above manually keyboarded speeds − up to fifteen lines of type a minute. This improvement obtains the best utilisation of the type-setting machine and allows several keyboards to produce setting for a single slug-casting machine.

The Intertype is also a slug-casting machine working on the same general principle as the Linotype, with machines for tape operation also available.

Slug-casting machines are widely − almost universally − used for letterpress newspaper production. The casting of the type in lines makes for rapid handling. Corrections are done by resetting the line in which the error has occurred. The quality of the printed impression obtained from slugs is, owing to the inflexibility of the lines of type, liable to be less even than with separate type characters. This does not matter much in the comparatively short measures to which the newspaper columns are set and, of course, the newspaper uses

Linotype slugs are produced from a keyboard which assembles matrices and adjustable spaces in due order from magazines. When the measure is nearly full the line is justified by forcing up wedge-shaped space bands between word-groups of matrices. Molten type metal is then injected into the justified line, so that, when cooled, a type-high slug is formed.

A development from manually-operated automatic typesetting machines is the tape-operated machine seen here. It does not need a keyboard and sets type at high speeds from tape punched on keyboards elsewhere in the plant. The machine shown is an Intertype Monarch.

a stereo or mould which is made from the type, so it is not the actual type produced by the composing machines which is impressed on to the paper in the printing press.

The classic type surface in separate movable characters, formerly available only from hand setting, is produced by the Monotype machine, in which a keyboard creates a perforated paper tape. The perforations are coded to operate a second machine, the caster, which does the actual moulding of the type. In this case the type is cast and composed, exactly as the hand compositor's work was, as separate type characters. Refinements in Monotype machines have extended the functions of the keyboard in many directions, notably those of setting mathematical and chemical formulae which requires 'shifts' in unit values and widths, and the capacity to set material which does not follow the straight line of text but may occupy any one of four different positions within the lines set. There are keyboards for an almost limitless range of characters and symbols, and special symbols can easily be incorporated on existing keyboards.

The above brief descriptions are adequate to show the efficiency and versatility of automatic composing machines and explain, at least in part, why the printer was reasonably content with his production methods for letterpress printing so long as the rest of his plant and machinery was organised on conventional lines. When discussing typesetting it is as well not to forget that the setting of type is not of itself a profit-making part of printing: it produces a printing surface as required by the letterpress process, but must precede the work for which the printer is more popularly recognised – the use of his presses in producing print. The amount of space taken up by a conventional 'hot metal'

A matrix case from a Monotype casting machine. The characters form moulds from which individual type characters are created out of hot metal.

Tape-perforating keyboard (in this case for Japanese characters) producing tape for automatic typesetting machinery.

composing room – by the type cases and furniture of hand-setting, by the line composing machines and casters and by the type itself in galley or in formes ready for the press – is considerable. So is the cost of employing trained compositors. Composition and correction are charged for in costing a printing job, but there is an obvious advantage to both printer and customer if this part of the printing sequence can be shortened, simplified or even eliminated altogether. The time taken in composing dictates, to a large degree, the loading of the presses and has an important bearing on the economical utilisation of printing machines.

Typesetting, by whatever method, must be carried out in accordance with the requirements of a given process. Thus, type composed in metal must, if it is to be used for one of the photographic means available for making printing plates, be proofed to provide the necessary positive for making a film image in the cameras. In the newer letterpress developments we have seen that many advantages can be secured by machines using a printing plate – either flat or curved – to improve production and performance at the replication stage. For offset the photographically produced printing plate is essential. In these and other cases typesetting in metal is not the final stage before reaching a printing surface. The newspaper printer takes a mould of the page in papier-mâché and uses this mould to cast his curved stereo for the rotary newspaper press. A duplicate of the type forme can be made in rubber or plastic to provide plates for letterpress machines using the rotary principle. But, on the whole, the main development has been towards circumventing the cumbersome business of typesetting in metal for platemaking which involves photo-mechanical reproduction methods.

The offset printer, who does not need a relief surface, was naturally the first to respond to photo-typesetting, which provided him with composition on film, ready for platemaking by photographic means. Again the development had to wait for the stimulus of demand and the availability of printing machinery which could use such new materials in the print shop. The use of a photographed image in place of metal type is recorded as long ago as 1876, and we can trace a similar progress through trial and error, acceptance and rejection in photo-typesetting as in automatic hot-metal line composing machines. A number of different photo-typesetting systems are now in use, ranging from those which replace the hot-metal caster with a unit which accepts keyboarded tape and produces, instead of metal setting, a roll of film which can be developed, cut, proofed and assembled along the same lines as the type forme was prepared, to fantastically high-speed machines

Monotype casters. These are used to cast metal type in galley form from perforated paper tape produced from keyboards.

capable of accepting computer-generated tape and setting characters at 6,000 per second such as the machine which set the text of this book.

At its simplest, photo-typesetting aims only at providing a finished piece of setting on film. The film, being less substantial than metal type, demands different skills for its manipulation and for the insertion of corrections. The commonest method for correcting is the use of film which adheres to a stronger transparent support, from which the film carrying the actual setting can be stripped away. Reset correction lines can thus be removed by cutting into the exposed and developed film and resetting, inserting the corrected lines on the stable base-film. (The two surfaces adhere immediately on contact.) Retouching and opaquing can be carried out directly on to the composed page. The film is the result of keyboarding and, with modern equipment, this part of the job has been simplified and speeded up. The keyboarding may contain coded instructions which are translated into typographic requirements in the setting.

Once keyboarded, with the added format instructions, the rest of the setting can be carried out by some equipment at very high speeds, automatically processed and made available as finished setting on film or photographic paper ready for use in the proofing and platemaking procedures which precede printing.

The general-purpose computer has also made its appearance in printing, and defining its functions at the typesetting stage of printing has taken up a good deal of time, talent and money. Here we see, once again, the impact of a highly developed technology – electronic

Corrections and alterations can be made on film by 'stripping in' the new material on to a transparent base support. The compositor uses a line grid as a guide and places the setting over it against a lighted background.

data processing – on the already highly developed technology of print itself. The people who design computers, peripheral equipment, systems and programs had to get to know a great deal about the thinking inside of the printing industry before there was any real communication between them and the printer. Not only this, they had to discover from the printer many of the whys and wherefores which lay behind his craft methods so that the work of skilled and trained craftsmen could be replicated in the systems designed for automatic processing via the computer. The trouble was (and still is) that, because many of the printer's typesetting procedures are conventions, he has never needed to analyse them in the precise terms required for computerisation. The very language of craftsman and technician differs, and the concepts of each can seem poles apart.

Here we come up against the nature of print rather than any purely technical or mechanical problem associated with its production. The photo-typesetting machine carried out – as did its predecessors the hot-metal composing machines – the setting of type in accordance with traditions which ensured conformity with existing typographical standards. Further, the printer was expected to provide authors with proofs, and continue in such other ways as he had in the past to supply the facilities which the letterpress process, in its original form, made possible. In short, the customer was prepared to allow

A panel of stripping film is separated with the scalpel during page make-up.

The Monophoto photo-typesetting machine which produces type on film. The machine is comparable to the hot-metal casting machine since it operates from a punched paper roll produced on a keyboard unit.

The 'master negative' is the equivalent of the matrix case on a hot-metal unit. It contains characters for use in the Monophoto photo-typesetting machine.

the printer to improve the efficiency of his service, provided he did nothing to disturb established procedures and results. It is true that the industry did not present the customer with very full or cogent arguments in favour of newer techniques, either from the stand-point of improved quality or reduced costs. But it must be remembered that the demands on the printing industry were fast becoming such that it was flexibility and output which became the prime needs. The new composing equipment and methods gave the printer advantages which were not always obvious to the individual customer, concerned only with his own piece of print. In the printer's world the photo-composing machine may have solved certain problems related to the expense and difficulty of setting in hot metal; but photo-typesetting, new platemaking methods, the use of computers and other such techno-logical developments do not wrench the printing industry into new paths so much as provide a means for the cautious improvement and extension of existing ones. They came on to the printing scene because they were needed for useful work and could reduce, in specific areas, some of the unprofitable or time-consuming methods used in the con-ventional plant.

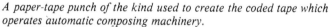

A paper-tape punch of the kind used to create the coded tape which operates automatic composing machinery.

The industry's problem, once alternatives were presented by new equipment and techniques of the sort I have described, was to define, first for its own purposes and then for its customers' information, what could and what could not be achieved by changes in production methods, bearing in mind that the criteria for the final product would be those which had always applied. Printers have not always done well in this task.

No doubt, given the right information, a mathematician could project a graph which would show the point at which the customer would recognise the advantages offered him by a specific development, such as photo-typesetting, and accept, for practical purposes, certain new limitations, either because it provided him with faster work, more flexible design, better quality or cheaper print. None of these customer advantages is inherent in the equipment itself, but many can be secured by the way in which it is used.

Ultimately, however, the customer may have a more profound choice to make: that between a printing industry which can still function economically, and therefore still cater for the whole gamut of printing requirements, or one which can no longer sustain itself because of its own forced dependence on uneconomical or out-of-date methods of production.

8 Typography and design: the craft of arrangement

Typography can be given either the wider connotation, which brings within its scope the arrangement and appearance on the page of *any* printed material, or, more narrowly, taken as the selection, arrangement and overall deployment of typeset matter, not including illustration, or any other non-typeset element in the printed page. I am personally in favour of keeping typography within the stricter definition, where it is concerned only with what the printer knows as 'type'. Typography is sometimes confused with type *design*, which is the designing of letterforms for casting by typefounders, but it has nothing to do with this: the typographer normally uses type which is already available in metal or on film; he selects, but does not directly create, a type design.

Such ground-clearing is necessary before we enter the labyrinth of typography and design, an aspect of printing which seems especially to interest the layman because it has to do with what is seen – the end result which can be judged visually and by reference to canons of taste and preferences.

Typography has often been called an art and, to the extent that the typographer uses his insight and imagination in the creation of a design, he is being 'artistic' in the popular sense of the word. The typographer and the creative artist are different, however, in that the typographer provides only a guide or plan from which the actual job of 'constructing' the work (typesetting and make-up) and producing a printed image (machining) is done. To my mind the typographer is closer to the industrial designer than he is to the artist. He does not decide content or function any more than do other industrial designers, but supplies the skills and knowledge needed to carry out the customer's intention successfully and in accordance with the uses to which the finished product will be put. He may enhance or obscure 'meaning' in a text, but does not supply such 'meaning'.

Distinctions of this kind need to be made before the considerable mystery which surrounds the activities of typographers and designers can be penetrated. The idea that a piece of type is either 'designed' or 'undesigned' is confusing. We tend now to think of typography and design as a specialised activity, separate from the more mundane tasks of production. Because print is commonly the product of machinery, it is easy to forget that *all* print starts with judgement and selection – design decisions of a kind – on the part of some of the craftsmen who help to produce it. You can design a plastic toy, set up a machine for its production, find an operator who can work the machine and press the button to make the required number of copies, all without involving the operative in anything approaching a design decision. But immediately you ask for something to be printed – be it nothing more than a single full point on a double-crown sheet – *somebody*

Type can be used as part of an abstract design in its own right.

has got to decide where the full point goes. You may get a typographer to decide, and the compositor will follow his directions as to the placing of the full point; or you may say 'all I want is a full point somewhere on the page' and leave the placing of it to the compositor. Either way this simple (and useless!) piece of print has been typographically 'designed' in the correct sense of the word.

For the greater part of the history of printing, printer and typographer were one and the same person. It would not have occurred to the generations of printers who followed Gutenberg, Wynkyn de Worde, Caxton, and other innovators, to have somebody around to tell them what to do with their type and what sort of appearance their pages should have. For this they had guides laid down long before printing was invented, or conventions dictated by the mechanical nature of the process – letterpress – which all printers then used. Not all this was 'typographic design' as we now use the term; a lot of it was tradition and rule of thumb. Yet it established, no less powerfully, the main traditions of typography – ones which still exert influence over the appearance of much of the print produced today, and over books in particular.

Before anybody takes these references to 'tradition' and 'convention' to indicate that hide-bound craft practices are standing lumpishly in the way of creativity, let them reflect on their own feelings when confronted by innovation in typographic design. Taking the book as the pinnacle of traditional typography, we recognise that it represents what we, the readers, want from a book page as much as what the typographer tries to give us. It does not require a knowledge of typography to recognise that some books are 'easier' to read than others, and what the reader finds 'easy' (in the sense of being easy on the eyes) has a lot to do with what he is used to – that which is familiar or, in other words, conventional.

The need for a familiar appearance as a basis for comprehension has been observed scientifically, and in *The Anatomy of Judgement*, by M. L. Johnson Abercrombie (Penguin Books), the author discusses comprehension of text and of the tendency, in seeing, 'to ignore or reject what does not fit in with the pattern'. He refers to a researcher into the psychology of seeing who concludes that a new object presented to the senses 'must also be *soluble in old experiences*, be *re*-recognised as like them, otherwise it will be un-perceived and uncomprehended'. These views are supported by a good deal of evidence, and are relevant to the very point we are making when we say that changes – sometimes quite small changes – in the appearance of print can lead to unexpected discoveries about the nature of seeing and understanding. Print is a medium of communication between author and reader. Apart altogether from our readiness or willingness to understand something, there seems to be an innate bar to comprehending that which our experience of similar material does not confirm.

It need hardly be said that the idea that typography is something which aims at embellishing a printed image is wrong. Typography should aid comprehension. One of the best books on the classical typographical tradition remains Beatrice Warde's *The Crystal*

Decorated types from Fournier's 'Manuel Typographique', 1764.

Goblet, a collection of essays first published in 1955. The title is taken from an analogy which the late Mrs Warde makes between typographic design and a crystal goblet. The goblet is a beautiful thing itself, and also a 'container' to hold a drink. When filled it is natural that we should be more interested in the content than the container, yet the latter, in its own way, subtly enhances the content while remaining 'invisible' unless we choose to see it 'for itself': yet the craftsmanship and care with which the goblet has been fashioned for our use have something to do with our pleasure in the content. This analogy with good typography has not been bettered, and can be explored with increasing subtlety and profit by anyone who wishes to clarify his ideas about what typography is 'for'.

Early printers had no special design problems: they were, in effect, in the 'antiques reproduction' business in so far as they were creating, with movable type, the appearance of books which had hitherto been handwritten, and doing so with an eye firmly fixed on the conventions of the scribe. The types cast by Gutenberg and his contemporaries were replicas of pen-formed characters, and many early books left spaces for initial letters and other decorative features to be put in by hand, the better to simulate the manuscript book.

It is interesting to notice how intact some manuscript conventions have remained when carried over to the printed book, and how many of them have persisted. For example, the initial letter, which scribes usually created with elaborate and traditional decorations as a natural extension of the penman's skill, was – after a period in which a space was left for the handcraft convention to continue – translated into type metal, and many foliated, historiated and other initials were cut for printers' use. Today we can still find vestiges of the tradition in the 'drop capital' which is sometimes used at the beginning of a chapter, though it now seems a rather pretentious device.

This small historical fact is less an example of the printer's resistance to change, or determination to hang on to outdated conventions, than his recognition, in commercial terms, that people want his products to look familiar. Caxton did not risk producing books which looked entirely different from their antecedents for similar reasons that the publisher and book printer of today will not readily depart from what he knows to be an accepted (therefore acceptable) appearance. The point was rammed home forcibly to the printer in the early days of printing when the printed book was regarded as a vulgar fake by many of those who, through privilege and learning, had grown to value and respect the manuscript book.

The present status of the typographic designer as a specialist in his own right stems from the proliferation of process and product which has made the printing industry so diverse in scope. To arrive at the correct estimate of what should go into a given item of print may need more intimate knowledge and detailed information about the purpose of the finished product than the printer might reasonably be expected to possess. Print is used, among other things, as an element in modern marketing, publishing, public relations, advertising and many other activities where decisions have to be taken on the way in which a single item of print fits in with wider policies and aims. Though the printer rarely, if ever, finds himself in the role of a passive carrier out of other people's orders, his contribution will normally be restricted to showing what can or cannot be done effectively with the equipment at his disposal.

The designer's preoccupation is with function, and with the means available to him to carry out the work economically and well. To do this properly he should be aware of the different processes, production methods and materials which provide him with his choice of possibilities, and select those which best accord with his client's or employers'

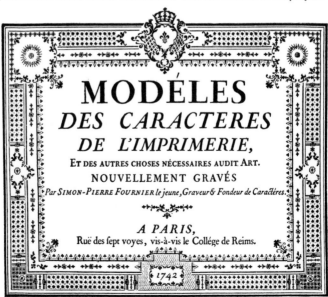

The title page of Fournier's first specimen book, printed by Joseph Barbou.

MODÉLES
DES CARACTERES
DE L'IMPRIMERIE,
ET DES AUTRES CHOSES NÉCESSAIRES AUDIT ART.
NOUVELLEMENT GRAVÉS
Par SIMON-PIERRE FOURNIER le jeune, Graveur & Fondeur de Caractéres.

A PARIS,
Ruë des fept voyes, vis-à-vis le Collége de Reims.

1742

intentions. Such a choice may be influenced by considerations other than aesthetic or technical ones: a long association with a particular printer could mean that a designer will deliberately create a design which that printer will find suited to his equipment. The advantage, to the designer, will be the speed and reliability which he knows he can expect. In other circumstances a designer may need to persuade a printer to experiment on his behalf with the aim of discovering the effect of particular design elements before the work is finalised. This often happens with the selection of papers; the number and variety of paper surfaces and weights is large, and their contribution to the appearance and quality of the finished article important. A printer may agree to proof a job on several papers, or with various colour inks, to enable a designer to reach a more informed conclusion on how the job should be done.

In this, and many other respects, the need for close liaison between designer and printer is demonstrated again and again. At worst the designer can, from lack of insight and knowledge of what is involved at the production stages of the job, make the printer's work more arduous and risky than it need be, even to the detriment of the work itself. And, on the printer's side, he may fail to communicate well with the designer, to understand the designer's problems or to carry out the intention behind the designer's instructions intelligently. Either way the need for a high level of understanding between those who design print and those who produce it is clear.

Bearing in mind that, in a basic sense, all print is designed by somebody, it would seem

Early stages in the design of a type face.

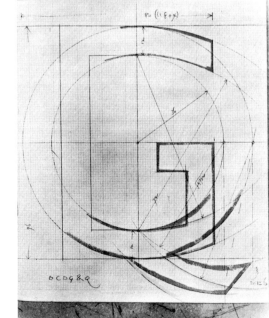

FAIRY REALM.

A COLLECTION OF

THE FAVOURITE OLD TALES.

ILLUSTRATED BY THE PENCIL OF

GUSTAVE DORE.

TOLD IN VERSE BY TOM HOOD.

LONDON:

WARD, LOCK, AND TYLER, 158 FLEET STREET,

AND

107 DORSET STREET, SALISBURY SQUARE.

A 'classic' title page, showing the sensitive and elegant disposition of different type elements arranged within the page. Note the careful letter-spacing of capitals and the use of punctuation, which is nowadays usually considered redundant in a title page.

common sense for the printer to become, once again, his own designer, or to employ a full-time designer. This is very often done, and many firms sell print and design as separate, but related, parts of the total service they offer to customers. The charges made for such a service may either be separated from the cost of the printing or integral with it. My own feeling is that design should always be charged separately, both for the customer's and the printer's satisfaction. The customer has, I believe, a right to know what part of the work which has gone into the whole job is 'design' and what it is costing him; the printer, by charging for a specific design, is helping to keep in the customer's view the need for specialised care, knowledge and skill in this area. It is only too easy for people just not to notice how well the designer has done his job (just as one may not notice the craftsmanship of the maker of the crystal goblet!); indeed, the better the design, in many fields of typography, the less obvious is the designer's contribution. We are helped by the designer to 'see' only the meaning, not the print, and, because nothing has been allowed to get between our eyes and the comprehension of the message or text, the design factor is ignored. It could be said, in many spheres of typography, that the 'visibility' of the printed word is evidence of the 'invisibility' of the typographer!

The design department which is part of a printing plant can offer certain advantages, but has some disadvantages from the customer's standpoint. The main advantage lies in the designer's intimate knowledge of all the equipment, and his estimate of what this, the labour force and other production elements, can and cannot achieve at a given moment. He will therefore fit his design accurately to the plant which is to produce the work and, beyond purely technical considerations, may also find short-cuts or economies which an outside consultant, however knowledgeable, would not know about. Provided his status within the company that employs him is established, the 'captive' designer can influence for the better the standard of craftsmanship and overall quality of the printing in a particular works. The disadvantages of the designer who works within a plant, compared with the outside consultant, are likely to be mainly in the sphere of originality and variety, and are roughly comparable with those between factory-made furniture and custom-designed furniture. Both can be efficient and pleasing, but the latter is more likely to show flair and originality. By designing print to fit the resources of a particular plant the designer must, if he is to be of value to his printer-employer, keep strictly within plant boundaries. These may not only include limitations imposed by process and machinery, but also by conditions in the factory at a given time – overloading or underloading of certain machines, for example. Such factors should not normally influence the design itself, and would not influence an independent designer who could easily choose to go to another printer if he discovered that the one he chose first could not meet his client's needs and his own requirements for the job in hand.

As usual, it is impossible to lay down rules, and a lot will turn on the characteristics of the work which needs to be done. A lot, too, depends on the amount of money to be spent. A printer may develop a design department which contains specialised knowledge which is

Claim your Gift at once by returning your Lucky Number Ticket today. 2,483 exciting prizes must be won-including a Luxury Cruise-for-Two aboard the QE2, "Dream" Kitchens, and Complete Home-Movie Kits!

Modern photographic techniques enable typographers to distort conventional types to a considerable degree.

not available elsewhere. For example, there is a printer who works for the motor-car industry and who employs a large design department staffed with artists and typographers who know a great deal about the techniques of designing literature for car manufacturers. The integration of this design expertise with the mechanical means of carrying out the work economically within the same plant makes it obviously an advantage for customers in this field to deal with a set-up so well equipped as to obviate the need for elaborate briefing on the design side. If the design element is complex (as it is, for example, in a great deal of magazine and poster advertising) a premium is placed on originality and inventiveness. Here again, there are companies who avoid the integrated design and print factory because they want to extract the maximum of variety and originality for their print by employing different designers with differing talents and a variety of approach. It is, unfortunately, easy to get stale or stereotyped when designing print, and while a specialist designer may solve most design problems to his own satisfaction in the specific area in which he works, it is unlikely that he will be able to produce, continuously, a stream of new ideas in those areas where originality and impact are always being demanded. This is the reason for the existence of so many freelance designers of print.

The call for originality is answered, to some extent, by the variety of typefaces available – a range which has been appreciably increased by photo-mechanical production methods, so that a new type design does not need to be cast in metal but may be photographed from drawn originals, transfer lettering or even from an ordinary printed specimen. The use of

BLACK CASUAL

SLIMBOY CAPS

CURLYCUE CAPS

ARIZONA

LIMEY CAPS

QUILL SHADED

SLIM DANDY

TOPPER topper

MOD BLACK mod black

Almost any letterform can be made available to printers using photographic methods of platemaking. These designs – some of them early and bizarre – are available from trade typesetters and are created either from proofed originals or redrawn from models. Photographic reproduction methods have given designers and printers access to many letterforms no longer available in founts of metal type.

film in place of metal also allows more scope for the designer in the free arrangement and positioning of his text, etc. Deliberate photographic distortion of letterforms can also be used.

It is convenient to take advertising design in newspapers and magazines as an example of an area where typographical originality is most often called for; here the advertiser (or his agent) is seeking to claim the reader's attention and hold it in competition with others who are trying to do the same thing. In the earlier styles of printed advertising it was usually assumed that the more an advertiser could say in a given space, the more persuasive would be his message. With today's volume of print, all of it trying to claim busy readers, the problem is not so much to get readers to assimilate your message, as to stop them from ignoring you altogether! Here a new factor is brought into the designer's craft. It may be that, by making a message more *difficult* to read he will gain attention, simply because people are curious as well as busy. We therefore get a number of tricks which, while they may not improve legibility in the classic sense, arrest attention by intriguing or puzzling the reader as he reviews the magazine.

It is hardly necessary to say that typography – if taken to be the disposition and arrangement of type – is only one element in advertising design and is inextricably involved with illustration by a variety of techniques. The advertisement takes its place on pages with photographs (in monochrome or colour) and the editorial text, which is what the reader has bought the magazine or newspaper for. So we discover that the classic imperatives of typography – legibility and clarity of overall design – are often modified or basically altered by new imperatives which call for a distinctive and distinguishing style of presentation at the cost, sometimes, of elegance, clarity and the more sober virtues of typographic design.

The distance which type designers have gone in supplying letterforms which, subtly or grossly, enhance, emphasise or merely make eccentric the simple basic forms of the letters of the alphabet can be seen by examining any of the larger catalogues of typefaces in the designer's armoury. There are fashions in type which are almost as ephemeral as fashions in women's clothing, designers moving from the severe to the ornate, from crudity to elegance, from assertiveness to understatement with apparent waywardness. Even in the less trendy world of book design there is scope for much variation within the conventional typographical elements.

Of course, type is not always used merely to enhance or to make distinctive a printed message. Different text types have different characteristics which fit them to one or another of the printing processes and to the papers on which they will print. A type (such as Bembo) in a specified text size may have refinements of design which would be lost if printed by high-speed letterpress rotaries from stereos on ordinary newsprint. The legibility of a text is further affected by such considerations as size in relation to line length (measure), letter spacing, word spacing and interlinear spacing (leading), all of which are centrally relevant to good typographical design. The contrast between the

Clearface Extra Bold no distortion

Clearface Extra Bold 20% condensed | Clearface Extra Bold 40% condensed

Clearface Extra Bold 20% expanded | Clearface Extra Bold 40% expanded

Clearface Extra Bold italicised | Clearface Extra Bold backslanted

Normal Spacing | V Close Spacing

Close Spacing | VV Close Spacing

British British British
Printer Printer Printer

Olly Twiddle is a gnome. Every Monday he goes to Gnome Town. He drives all the way. He doesn't drive the new Ford Anglia. Naturally, he drives a much smaller car.

Women grow lovelier at sea.

Using film in place of metal type allows more flexibility in design. These examples show what can be done to order by trade typesetters who supply printers with film ready for platemaking.

colour of the type and the colour of the printed surface is equally important in the designer's search for optimum legibility or impact (though, oddly, this is often a neglected element, and it is surprising how many designers are unable to notice in time that black type on a dark coloured paper, or reversed out against an eye-catching half-tone is difficult to read).

The page – whatever size it may be – may be regarded as a frame inside which must be disposed all the elements required for the reader's comprehension and assimilation, and format is the first concern of the typographer. The second could well be process, which

Metal type is the tool of the typographer. It is made in a foundry and cast to highly accurate dimensions. This type has just been cast and awaits assembly into complete founts.

will determine what possibilities are open to him and what limitations he must observe. The third could be materials – papers, inks, method of binding, where needed, and any of the many finishing operations which may be called for to suit the print to its intended use. So it can be seen that, in its wider implications, typographic design has to go well ahead of the actual selection of typefaces and their arrangement on the paper if it is to do its job properly. Indeed, the designer, in some fields, needs to relate his work to a wider intellectual context where social or psychological principles may be worth considering as contributing to a typographic end. He is influenced by all kinds of extraneous things, as, for example, the speed of traffic (in poster design), the popularity of television (in the selection of pictures), the nature of the product (as when using type to give a feeling of weight or lightness, strength or delicacy, dignity or impudence to the printed message).

The fact that typography and graphic design are so often treated separately from printing is evidence of the increasing need for a specialised approach to design problems as distinct from production conditions. At worst the two become physically separated and the designer works in a vacuum without knowledge of, or reference to, the final result which has to be achieved by the techniques of the commercial print factory. Methods of training graphic designers are often such that the student gains more insight into the use of pens, pencils and brushes than film and metal, machines and methods, so that by the time he is judged ready to enter his profession he has lost sight of the practical considerations which should, to a large extent, dictate the nature of the design solutions he offers. There is also a struggle for status among designers which, though not itself a bad thing, can occasionally become manifest in deliberate mystification or mere faddism. A lot can depend on the clarity with which those who use the services of designers can bring to defining their own wishes and objectives; in short, the purpose of print must be largely defined by the customer, while the means for its realisation must be discovered by designer and printer together. This three-way communication is by no means easy to control, but a *modus operandi* has to be found every time a new piece of printing is initiated. A failure to do so is not always obvious, since it is hard to know with any exactness just how many readers have assimilated a printed message and how easy, or how difficult, it was for them to do so. For this reason alone, one suspects that a good deal of effort is wasted in the field of typographic design, but it is virtually impossible to decide precisely where really hard-working design stops and the rest begins.

9 Illustration and reproduction

With illustration – particularly coloured illustration – printing was finally and decisively emancipated from the strict conventions of text. Some kind of printed illustration had always been feasible, even before the invention of movable type: the wood block provided a relief surface for multiplication by impression and was used for illustration, as it is today. But early printing was sparing and often crude in illustration and, until the printed word came into demand by a popular readership, words were considered more valuable than pictures in the printed page. The early broadsheets show a change, and printers were able to sell woodcuts showing, in fine imaginative detail, the murders, executions and other sensations which diverted the public of the sixteenth and seventeenth centuries much as they do now.

Illustrated print of the quantity and quality we find today can be dated from the invention of photography and the speedy developments which followed in providing the printer with photo-mechanical means for making a block, or printing plate, which he could use with type. Lithography was, at its inception, a process well suited to illustration: the lithographic stone was a drawing surface for reproducing an inscribed image. The offset printing plate is made photographically, and is consequently receptive of the photographic image without intermediate manipulation and, of course, photogravure has in its very name the clue to the method used in this process to obtain a printing surface.

Once methods for making photographs into printing plates were available, the progress towards modern colour printing was rapid. Techniques of multi-colour reproduction were long established and had, in various places and at various times, reached considerable refinement (as in the Japanese wood-block print, which was sometimes overprinted in as many as eight or more colours).

The Victorians, with a number of well-developed techniques for illustration at their disposal, invented the 'picture book', which existed for its illustrations alone, and there are many fine examples of colour printing in line and tone from this period. The arrival of the photo-mechanical half-tone block rapidly extended the possibilities for printed illustration via the camera, and increasingly varied and accurate techniques of colour reproduction have sustained the picture book at a high level of popularity. Illustration is possible in all three main printing processes, though the gravure process has proved most successful in providing good-quality colour reproduction at a low price for a mass market.

Illustration, from the simple line block to the multi-colour art print, is so extensive and varied a part of print that it is unnecessary to count its many manifestations in modern printing: it can be seen all around us, from the postage stamp to the poster. The printer is constantly called upon to reproduce the appearance of things. He has, therefore, many techniques at his disposal, and has adapted these to a market which has unquestionably decided that twopence coloured is better than penny plain.

Before such techniques are described, however, a few points might usefully be made about printed illustration in general. An original must be created, or already exist; but the *print* created from the original is quite a different matter. Self-evident though this may seem, even experienced buyers of print have been known to call for fidelity in printed reproduction to colour transparencies which contain both a sharpness and purity of colour which printing processes cannot emulate. The most obvious difference between an original and a printed reproduction is between the materials of which the two are made. Colour film uses dyes supported on a film base; print uses inks supported on a paper base. Colour transparencies are viewed by transmitted light, while print is viewed by reflected light. The base colour, surface finish and reflectance of a paper, and the printing process used, affect the colours seen by the viewer. The colour quality of the light under which the print is viewed has a similarly direct effect on colour values, as do the inks themselves. It is consequently unreasonable to make exact comparisons between photographic and printed reproductions, though the latter has means of compensating for deficiencies in the former, and can often improve on poor originals. Nevertheless, 'good' and 'poor' colour is, at some levels, as much a subjective matter as one capable of objective measurement.

Because colour comparison, with its subjective elements of what different people see, is a recurring problem in illustration, efforts have been made to obtain standards of one kind and another which are designed to achieve a measure of agreement between what is meant by 'colour' in printing. A colour intensity can be measured with a densitometer, which provides the printer with a scale of measurements which can be translated into chemical or mechanical adjustments in inks and press settings, and colour blocks or patches are often printed alongside a sheet so that the densitometer can be used accurately to measure and analyse the colour characteristics of strength (density) and hue (reflectance) in the actual print. The trouble (as I have already indicated), is in what people *expect* of colour. A printer may use more or less sophisticated methods of arriving at exact colour comparisons between original and printed reproduction, but may be confused by ambient conditions when such comparisons have to stand up to the subjective appraisal of his customer.

It was not until 1931 that a standard of illumination for daylight viewing for colour matching was established. It was an unsatisfactory standard, and in 1960 a BSI committee responsible for the standardisation of artificial daylight values for colour matching was reconstituted. It was 1963 before an internationally agreed standard (D 6500) was published, and 1965 before manufacturers could be persuaded to produce an illuminant suitable for standard viewing. The problem, it must be emphasised, is that of viewing, under standard conditions, two quite disparate systems of colour reproduction – the

*Accurate measurement of colours over the various parts of a colour print are
necessary for today's precise methods of reproduction. Colour densitometers
provide the printer with measured values on the surface of the actual picture.*

transparency (produced photographically and reproduced in dyes formulated for photographic transparency reproduction) and the 'flat' print, which must be viewed by reflected
light, screened and overprinted and reproduced in printing inks, with the paper itself
playing an important part in the visual strength of the colours. Viewing cabinets are now
available for such controlled comparisons, and, it should be noticed, comparisons need to

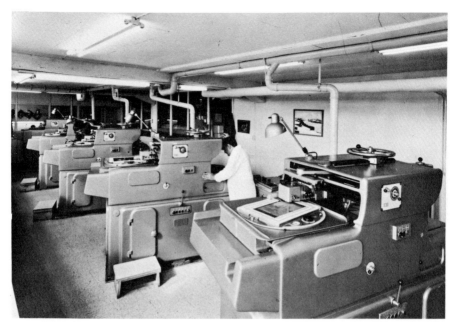

A Vario-Klischograph, showing rotatable picture-table with vacuum frame and scale for screen rotation, colour optics head with adjustment wheels for colour correction filters and diaphragms.

An electronic scanner which produces colour separations as required for multi-colour printing.

be made at several stages along the route to the final print: they may be made as direct comparisons between the colour of the objects photographed and the resulting transparencies (as when a sample of a furnishing fabric is used for direct comparison with the photograph). The standardised colour comparison should also be made by the photoengraver who makes the blocks or separation negatives and proofs them for the printer (ideally on a paper identical to that on which the job is to be run); and, finally, the printer needs to make exact comparisons between the original photograph and the products of his press, the settings and inks of which can be adjusted to give the most accurate rendering of colours. This kind of procedure obviates the vagueness associated with looking at colours in lighting conditions which affect the viewer's judgement of what he is, in fact, seeing. The 'side-by-side' comparison of transparencies and 'flat' printed sheets under standard lighting conditions is probably the most practical way of securing agreement as to what the colours ought to look like. Densitometric measurement, and the production of standard colour swatches, keyed for visual comparison, are both subject to question at those stages of the job where what the printer and his customer sees are affected by the differing lighting conditions under which viewing is carried out.

Monochrome reproduction presents fewer measurement problems. The tonal gradations of a white-to-black picture are commonly reproduced by screens which break the picture down into dots or lines. The number of dots or lines used in screening varies and affects fidelity of tonal gradations, but in all screened monochrome reproduction the appearance of the final printed image is more a matter of illusion than reality. Take a magnifying glass to any newspaper half-tone and it is quite easy to see the image as constructed of white paper and inked dots. The human eye and brain are conditioned to accept this interpretation of tonal values, both in monochrome and colour, from the information derived from a 'broken-up' image on the page, though we may need greater or lesser visual adjustment, depending on the nature of the information. All other things being equal, a printed picture on art paper which has a very smooth surface and high reflectance has to be printed with finer screen (number of dots per square inch) than a picture on coarser paper if the illusion of continuous tone is to be obtained.

The printer uses separate printing surfaces (plates) for the different colours which combine to make a finished print. Let us contemplate the problem in its pure form: a scene comprising many colours, tones and hues is photographed on a sunny day. It is already questionable whether two people standing together and looking at the scene see exactly the *same* colours. But if a photograph is taken the wide range of colours is compressed into the three or four colours of the dyes used to produce the image of the scene. A basic set of 'primary' colours combine to approximate those of the original scene. If these photographic dyes are used to produce four printing plates which recombine the colours – now seen as printing inks one above the other (with white and black) – to reproduce the original scene, it is not surprising that we have moved, in many directions, quite a long distance from the original colour values.

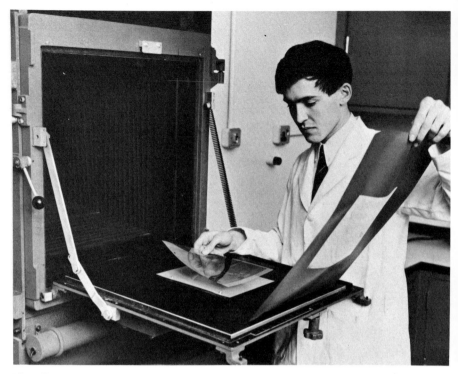

The offset process demands separation negatives for multi-colour printing. These are made photographically by techniques which mask the different colour components of a multi-colour picture so that separate printing plates can be made for the separated colours, which will eventually be printed successively and in register.

Absolute fidelity to nature is therefore impossible. More interesting, for those who create print as designers or printers and use it as consumers, is the degree to which people *can* accommodate to, or ignore, the limitations of printed colour. At a very early age we interpret the crude colours of the comic book without discomfort or question, and by the time we have handled much print as an everyday thing we have made practically all tne compromises and subjective corrections necessary to accept the wide range of colour discrepancies between natural objects and their appearance on the printed page. This does not mean that the printed image can always neglect fine tonal gradation, shade and hue, but it does provide a set of criteria which calls for a sensible estimate of what values can and cannot be achieved in the final effect of a particular piece of print. A reproduction of a painting in an art gallery will *never* replicate the quality and variety of tone and surface which an artist achieves with oil-paints, but can attain, with just four or six colours, a quite remarkable verisimilitude if the reproduction is conscientiously and skilfully done. Here the criterion is easily found, for we have a graphic original to which the print may directly be compared. Occasionally we can discover how completely the average person has grown accustomed to accepting printed colours as exact: the printing of mail order catalogues poses special problems of colour matching where fabrics are chosen and ordered from printed reproductions; the buyers naturally want the goods to look as much like the pictures as possible. The difference between the colours obtained by fabric dyes and printing inks may be obvious, but they are academic to the woman who has ordered a dress in a particular coloured pattern which, on arrival, has a different set of tonal values from the one depicted in the catalogue. She will doggedly insist that the dress be 'the same' as that shown in the catalogue illustration.

A characteristic common to letterpress and offset, when reproducing illustration, is that the inks are deposited on the paper in uniform thickness and as *discontinuous* (i.e. screened) films. Collotype (*q.v.*) is an exception, and is also capable of applying inks of graduated thickness, as is gravure. There are some specialised techniques for varying the thickness of the inks in letterpress and lithography, but it can generally be assumed that the mechanics of reproduction do not allow the 'building up' of colour which the artist uses to obtain certain effects and to intensify a colour already on the paper. In printing, therefore, the inks must be chosen and combined for an *immediate* colour match under the conditions of a press run.

Originals for line and half-tone photography may be black and white for either mono-chrome or coloured reproduction. Line drawings are scaled for reproduction, photo-graphed, retouched if necessary and exist, in this form, ready for gravure cylinder or platemaking by one or other of the methods available to the different processes. The half-tone processes all aim at the conversion of continuous-tone images into a pattern of controlled-size dots which, when printed and viewed at the customary distance, give an illusion of continuous tone. The cross-line screens used to break up the image into a specified number of dots are ruled and then placed one above the other; the resulting 'grid' provides the required dot coverage. A 55-line screen is somewhat coarse, an 85- to 110-line screen above average, and screens ruled to provide 133 lines and over are considered 'fine', since they admit greater detail into the screened image. The screen is placed between the lens of the process camera and the sensitised surface of the paper or film. The opaque grid is therefore transferred to the sensitised surface on exposure.

The methods of photo-engraving or gravure cylinder preparation, or offset litho plate-making, together with the inbuilt characteristics of papers and inks and the settings possible on the presses themselves, all add up to an impressive range of 'controls' by which verisimilitude is obtained in illustration. So important is this flexibility in the reproduction of printed pictures that the industry has, perhaps, overloaded itself with options. The most technically advanced system is judged in much the same way as the more primitive or simple systems – by the eye and the imagination of the viewer – and, for the future, the printing industry, with its associated techniques of photo-engraving, may need to settle down with a range of controls more automated and less dependent on the judgement and skills of craftsmen on the production side than is now the case. There are various automatic systems for the preparation of the separate negatives required for making the three, four or more colour sets of plates needed for offset colour printing, and automatic systems for the creation of half-tone blocks for letterpress. There are also standards for process colours and the inks themselves. All have in common the 'mechanical' interpretation of measured colour standards, from originals through the various stages to the final printing surface. But all stop short of the conditions which arise *during* printing. They may therefore be considered as aids to the printer (just as line composing machines mechanically aid him in producing text setting, which is nevertheless judged, in its final appearance on the paper, by the same criteria as the earlier methods of hand composition) and have to do with the costs of production. The efforts made to reduce the cost of colour printing rarely have much to do with the sort of satisfaction we derive from looking at a fine piece of colour reproduction, the value of which still resides in the techniques and skills brought to bear on the various stages of its production.

10 Computers in print

It should by now be abundantly clear that no isolated development in printing can be decisive in changing the whole industry fundamentally and quickly: the interrelationship of methods and techniques and of machinery and materials within the printing processes is elaborate. Since printing is a *sequence* of operations, it can be materially assisted by anything which has the effect of speeding up or improving specific parts of that sequence, bearing in mind that the ultimate purpose is to make printed impressions; therefore the product – print – is a matter for the presses, and their speed is the determining factor in making the material available to the reader. This does not mean that press speeds cannot be improved (this will certainly happen), or that some print is not more quickly processed than some other: the daily newspaper is an obvious example of how quickly information can be disseminated when production is geared entirely to one category of print, even when conventional methods are used. It would, however, be a mistake to assume that, by introducing high-speed methods of composition into printing, the sole – or even the main – aim is increased speed in obtaining printed impressions. The concentration on composition by advanced technology has been directed towards something more subtle than the goal of speed alone. If the stages between original copy and a printing surface can be simplified, standardised, speeded or *in any other way* made cheaper or easier, the printing industry is ready to listen, provided the product is one which can be sold in one or another of the printers' many markets. This is not as obvious as it may first appear. I have already spent some time discussing the innate conservatism of readers and users of print, and it is relevant to any new development that most, if not all, the wide and varied needs of readers should be contained within its repertoire of possibilities.

There are certain large categories of print where even a marginal advantage in the costs of production can become important due to the quantity of material handled. The example of the newspaper plant is again useful: if its product were anything other than newspapers – if, for example, the machines were needed for different categories and sizes of printed material of different lengths of run – it would be difficult to use the methods of newspaper production profitably for all requirements. But, given a single main product (in this case a newspaper), plant and techniques can be tailored quite accurately to efficient production at high speeds, and even small improvements will materially affect the efficiency of the production side.

This should be true of any equipment or system which occupies a place in printing. Computers are used principally in typesetting and, in considering their functions and value to the printer, the foregoing must be recognised. It may be necessary here to say that

An operator at the keyboard of a photo-composing system which works direct to the photo-typesetting machine. The controls are under operator-decision and the typewriter print-out allows the operator to see what is being supplied as input to the photo-composer. The keyboard unit contains a small special-purpose computer to implement typographic decisions, but no general-purpose computer is involved and, therefore, no specially designed typographic program is needed apart from that incorporated in the keyboarding unit itself.

computer typesetting is not, as is often implied, something which lies in the future for printing. There are already a large number of computer typesetting installations in Europe, but the United States printing industry has taken a decisive lead in this field. A survey conducted at the end of 1968 showed a 54 per cent growth in computer typesetting installations in America in a single year, and the number of users is given as 821, 287 of these being new installations. The graph of computer users in printing works (for type-setting alone) rose from below 50 at the beginning of 1964 to 800 five years later.

What does a computer do in a printing works? It does not set type. The commonest use to which computers are put is of introducing into keyboarded tape a number of format and typographical needs which will determine the appearance of the printed text. The computer input is text setting on tape; the output is coded tape including format and typographical instructions. Just as the compositor, by hand or machine, has to think of the text as type in a specified typeface of a certain size, of a certain line length and with all the

The input to a computer-aided typesetting system can be monitored at the keyboard stage with a screen which shows the operator what is contained on the punched tapes. This is of value when (as in the picture) a second 'corrections' tape is being keyboarded. The corrections are later merged to provide a 'clean' tape for final setting.

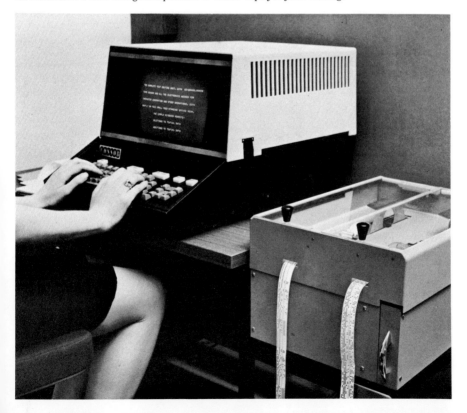

spacing, word-breaks, italics, capital letters and other textual conventions included, so the computer program must apply such of these requirements as are needed to convert 'straight' input ('idiot tape' as the experts picturesquely call it) into typographically stylised output. The computer, therefore, contains within its stored program all, or most, of the *typographical* 'decisions' which an experienced compositor takes as a result of his knowledge and experience of typesetting. This is a drastic simplification of the computer's role, but it serves to indicate two important things: that the program may be written to produce a particular *kind* of text setting – e.g. for a newspaper or a series of paperback books of given size and style – and that the product of the computer – its output of paper tape – can be used to control the actual typesetting equipment, including conventional automatic composing machines using hot metal, or any photo-typesetting system. The output of the total system – typesetting which is ready for making into a printing surface – is therefore dependent on the program employed.

A distinction is necessary between two main types of equipment available for computer typesetting. The first category uses relatively small special-purpose computers designed to accept and process input from a keyboard supplied with a number of instructions, including some which can be applied by the operator. In this type of system the overall needs of text composition have been studied and certain 'fixed' elements, such as typeface selection, line length, changes of typeface, line justification, etc, are established before setting is started so that, while these remain under operator control, the actual operations are carried out by the processor automatically. The keyboard operator pre-sets these requirements as constants for a given piece of setting and proceeds to keyboard his copy with the assistance of a number of 'instruction' keys which can control or modify the input and, therefore, the output. For example, if a text requires bold face or italic for a single word, or if footnotes in a smaller type-size are occasionally demanded, it is at the keyboard stage that the necessary instructions must be given to ensure the production of an output tape which includes them; it is the input from the keyboard *and* the output from the computer which drives the typesetting equipment itself.

Such keyboards may be arranged so that several work directly to a single computer, processing the input data and providing output for composing equipment as a centralised operation. Alternatively, the keyboards may be set up to produce only paper tape (or magnetic input tape in some rare instances), which, at any future time, may be used as input to a computer. The computer, therefore, does not necessarily have to be linked physically with the keyboard in all instances.

Where keyboards and computer are kept apart the advantages are probably with the second main type of computer composition referred to, namely the use of a general-purpose computer into which any number of different typographical programs may be read and stored. The basic principles of electronic data processing are nowadays sufficiently widely understood to make it unnecessary, at this juncture, to break off and spend time describing them: it is sufficient for our purposes if we know that computers

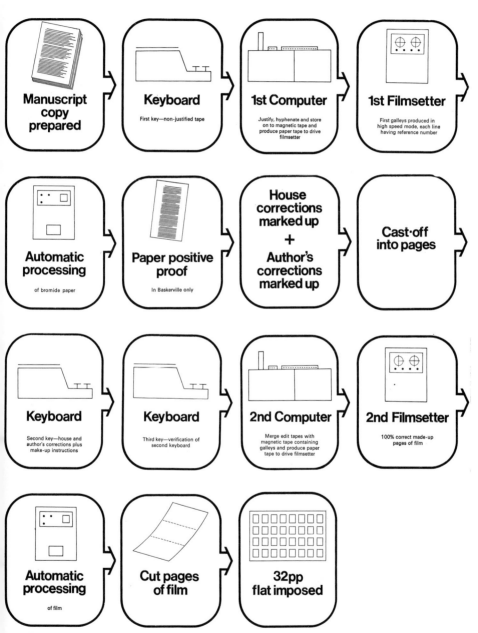

Diagram of a sequence in which original text can be processed by a computer typesetting system.

are, in essence, machines which can carry out arithmetical calculations in accordance with a set program, and can store and retrieve such information in a programmed sequence. The programs used in computer typesetting do not differ in principle from those used for many other computer operations; that is to say, the computer 'obeys' the programmer's instructions by performing a series of calculations in accordance with the needs of the output, which in this case is tape used to operate a typesetting machine. It follows that what exists as text must be keyboarded in the precise terms required by the computer program. This presents few initial difficulties if input codes are assigned unit values, so that the positions they occupy in the desired format can be manipulated by arithmetical computations. For occasional instructions, such as those needed to 'command' capital letters, italics and other typographical details in the text, little computation is really necessary once the appropriate instruction has been input and transferred by the computer to the output tape. The general-purpose computer, therefore, is used principally to maintain surveillance over input and translate such input into a given style and format. In short, you do not really need a computer to 'put in' such 'typography' as can normally be incorporated by the simple controls of an ordinary typewriter keyboard. The important difference between what can easily and quickly be keyboarded, using a keyboard capable of making a punched tape, and what, in print, is considered necessary beyond this basic function is the balance taken up by computation.

Diagram of a computer typesetting system. Here the copy is taken from the 'input perforator' stage; the diagram shows how input can bypass correction and hyphenation units and be routed to those computer units required. The system is designed to provide output of paper tape of two different kinds, one for the operation of Monotype machines, either photo-composing or hot-metal, and another for producing paper tape coded for other kinds of hot-metal or high-speed photo-typesetting machines.

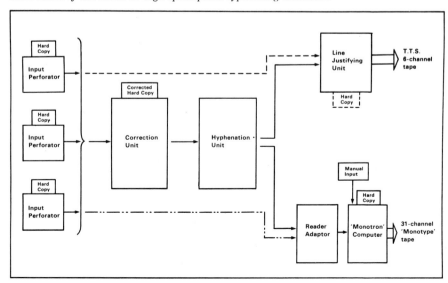

Here we are concerned with calculation – the true realm of the computer – and the calculation, in this case, is primarily one of spatial arrangement or, to use the printer's term, format. There is in this field a prime requirement which the computer which processes tape for typesetting must provide: justification. Justified type – type which has even right- and left-hand margins – is obtained by two methods, one the introduction of variable spacing between words to bring the lines out to the correct length for an even right-hand margin, and secondly, the breaking of words where such means will not give reasonably close word spacing. (A third method can be employed in photo-composition, where type can be optically distorted – expanded or condensed – to take up the extra space which may be needed to justify a line; but this is of strictly limited use, since the typeface itself, and the correct spacing between individual letters in a word, should be exact, and excessive distortion of either will quickly detract from the good appearance and legibility of the text.)

A computer can be programmed to carry out all the calculations needed to establish word spacing within acceptable limits and, beyond these, when a word break is required, to break the word and place part of it in the next line. But it is much more difficult to give the computer some means of determining exactly *where* a given word should be broken. Most readers do not realise that printers have a set of rules for word breaking which assist the easy assimilation of text in continuous reading. The *Rules for Compositors and Readers at the University Press, Oxford*, first compiled in 1893 and now in its 37th revised edition, states, 'Avoid divisions if at all possible, having regard to the requirements of typography (even spacing, etc). Not to inconvenience the reader must always be one of the main considerations.' Compositors are advised to divide words according to their etymology (e.g. atmo-sphere, bio-graphy) or, where such etymology is not immediately apparent, according to pronunciation (e.g. abs-tract, minis-ter). Two consonants forming one sound, as in calm-est or debt-ors, are pointed out, and there follows a long list of rules all designed 'not to inconvenience the reader'. The compositor has no difficulty in recognising word-break situations and applying the rules in accordance with his training. The computer, on the other hand, is not trained but programmed: it can accomplish only what the program specifies. Given an exact ruling, the programmer can translate this into instructions for the computer. What such instructions cannot, however, embody are all the exceptions and variations needed to ensure 100 per cent accuracy in word breaking over the whole language. Word breaks such as 'leg-ends' for 'legends,' 'read-just' for 'readjust' or 'reap-pear' for 'reappear' do not help the reader; they stick out like sore thumbs.

In the type of equipment described earlier in this chapter, where the operator has direct control or 'converse' with the computer, the word-break situation is kept under surveillance during the actual keyboarding, and a number of devices are used which enable the operator to see and decide where a word can be broken for correct justification and proper word-breaking. In one such system a word which overruns the required measure is automatically displayed on a screen and the operator uses his input keys to instruct the computer where to break. In such systems the operator may be able either to reassign word spacing to secure a justified line or key instructions as to where the word may be broken. In the case of the general-purpose computer the operator is probably in direct correspondence, or two-way contact, with it. The computer program must therefore contain all (or as many as possible) of the rules needed to secure accurate word-breaking. In practice, this has not proved as difficult as it first seemed to be. Programming techniques and the expanded storage capacity of modern computers have largely overcome the problem, though it has remained a point for discussion not only between printers who wish to use computers for justified text setting but also between those who are questioning the true validity of many of the printer's typographical conventions (such as text justification) which have been carried over from the days of hand composition via automatic composition into today's computer-assisted photo composition. In normal computer typesetting practice the demand for accurate word-breaking uses up a large enough part of the basic typographic program to concern those anxious to economise on storage space.

The most appropriate use to which a computer can presently be put in printing is in the preparation of lists and similar tabulated matter where constant updating is called for and where typography and format is consistent within definite limits. Air-line time-tables, telephone directories and tax tables are examples of the kind of printing which can be handled extremely efficiently by computerised methods. The main advantages here lie more in the ability of the computer to 'update' existing information than in its output for primary typesetting. A book or list can be set and, since the setting exists as computer output, later changes, insertions and variations in content can be keyboarded when a new updated text is required. This is simple data handling and, when input to the computer, the corrections can be automatically incorporated in a fresh tape, with the amendments merged, without the need for rekeyboarding the whole of the setting. Large quantities of such material can be stored conveniently in the form of punched tape, or on magnetic tape, for use when revised and updated versions of an original text are required.

Indeed, it has been found possible to provide computers with all the information needed to process and output for typesetting without *any* keyboarding. In such cases a computer generates the primary information, as it does, for example, in calculating tax tables or producing mathematical tables. Purely numerical computation of this kind does not involve written text, and the primary output may be channelled directly to a computer typesetting system, without keyboarding, for the incorporation of all the necessary instructions (by a typographical and formatting program) for producing a tape to obtain the pages of figures to be set by a typesetting installation.

The value and importance of computers in printing has led to some distortion and exaggeration of their functions. We are accustomed to being impressed by the immense speeds of automatic data processing but, when these are applied to printing, it is one thing being able to set text at extremely high speeds and quite another to produce the plates and the print itself, which is the aim and object of the exercise. It is not detracting from the advantages which computer typesetting has brought to printing to point out some of the more obvious blind alleys into which it can lead both expert and layman.

As I have already implied, to set the complete works of Shakespeare in a few seconds may be impressive, but to have the complete works of Shakespeare available for reading as a book depends on typesetting, platemaking, printing and binding, which may appreciably extend the time-span of the operation. The actual time used for the data-processing part of the operation may be infinitesimal, but, just as we must not forget what follows, we must also remember that, in most commercially available computer typesetting systems, the time needed for the *origination* of input by keyboarding is not substantially less than it would be if carried out by an experienced compositor on conventional equipment. There is, then, little to recommend the elaboration and expense of computers in printing works unless careful attention has been paid to the part they are to play in the *total* sequence of operations which have to be carried out there. Computers, in this context, are concerned *only* with typesetting, and it is a matter of utmost concern that their contribution in this area should be measurable against the whole of the productive effort involved. The question must be, first, 'what goes into the computer and what comes out?' If the answer is 'all kinds of text typesetting' it will certainly be necessary to go further by finding out what typographical denominators can be found which are common to all such input.

A printer whose typesetting is mainly for book production may find it possible to use a computer-assisted system with certain provisos. These may mean a reduction in the number of alternatives offered in typographical style, illustration and availability of proofs and correction compared with more conventional means. A computer may use any one of many different typographical programs, but the value of computer composition lies in its ability to automate and simplify time-consuming decisions, and its facility in handling material already set (as in the up-dating routines already described). There is also clearly a gain in space, efficiency and the amount of craft-based skills needed compared with the methods of the conventional composing room. But, once again, do not forget that the computer does not set type, and the printer is faced with a decision as to what, in fact, should set the type which his computer has processed.

Here we come into the realm of composition, which has been dealt with separately in Chapter 7. If the computer output is used to operate conventional equipment there will be a rapid increase in the amount of time required before keyboarding can be realised in terms of metal type in the galley. The computer's ability to handle, at high speed, large quantities of input may, in this case, be sufficient compensation to the printer whose problem is *setting* (i.e. keyboarding) capacity: a number of keyboards (not necessarily in the same place as the computer) can be made to work directly to one computer, which applies all the typographical requirements within its programmed capability for use as and when needed.

A more likely solution to the handling of computer output is to employ one or another

A character disc from a photo-typesetting system made by Harris-Intertype.
The disc is transparent and spins continuously. The characters and spacing are 'flashed' on
to film from a light source triggered by input tape from a computer after keyboard
origination.

of the high-speed photo-typesetting machines which will rapidly translate the computer output into setting on film. Here the close interrelationship of equipment and process is again demonstrated. If, due to the considerations of typesetting, the product at the end of the composing stage is film there is a strong argument in favour of using a printing process which employs film as its means of producing a printing plate – i.e. offset lithography. There now develops a need to balance the pros and cons of the printing process itself with the product of the typesetting system which must precede it.

Finally – and essentially – the customer must be considered. He will not be impressed, where a highly sophisticated typesetting system is used, if this means paying the same, or more, to get exactly the service and results that he got from a conventional system. Nor will he readily settle for a drastic reduction in the amount of choice he and his customers may have in obtaining specific kinds of setting, format, size, quality and so on. If he is accustomed to receiving galley and page proofs for correction he may still demand them. Here we are concerned with the buyer of the print and not necessarily with the consumer: it may not matter to a reader whether the book he buys reaches a given requirement as to size or typographical format, provided his reading habits are not disturbed by radical differences between the book he gets from the use of new setting methods and the books to which his reading habits have made him accustomed. However, the buyer of the printer's product – in this case the publisher – may have more specific needs. To find out what readers, buyers of print and printers hope for from computer typesetting, it is necessary to return to the equipment itself.

Most general-purpose digital computers have a 'printout', which means that they automatically produce, in readable form, the information contained in the output (which, of course, is simply a perforated tape). This printout is both legible and capable of being used directly to make a plate for printing. The differences between a computer printout and the product of a typesetting machine are many and obvious. The former is usually all

This central computer system handles incoming setting from remote terminals for processing and typesetting newspapers in Holland. Setting originating from Amsterdam and The Hague is handled in Rotterdam, where the newspapers are printed.

in capital letters, and may also contain additional letters or symbols used as codes to 'instruct' the computer program in one or another of its functions. Obviously, then, a computer printout is less than is needed by the printer for his customers. Its value, however, lies in being, at this stage, the only *visible* evidence of what has passed through the computer. (Such a printout is normally available only from a general-purpose computer. With the special-purpose equipment designed for setting directly from keyboards the printout is replaced by the typewritten copy produced at the keyboard simultaneously with the keyboarding of input. This exhibits most of the characteristics of a computer printout, though it will probably be more easily read and be written in the customary 'upper and lower case' letters [capitals and miniscules].)

In either case the printout is a kind of proof, and can be roughly equated with a galley proof taken from type metal. The difference between the two is important, however: to correct the computer printout properly one needs to be familiar with its conventions, which differ from those of the proofed galley. It may, for instance, be necessary to know input codes for paragraphing, capitalisation, typeface changes, etc, which, to the uninstructed reader of the printout, appear as arbitrary symbols (it is possible, in some systems, to differentiate between the actual text and the codes by using a different colour

Typewriter composition also uses computer controls. The operator is monitoring the transfer of 'standing copy' (in the form of paper tape) on to an automatic typewriter at a speed of up to 80,000 characters an hour. For updating or alteration to the original input the operator can stop the transfer of type and insert new copy at any point.

for the latter). Surprisingly few people are prepared for this. Publishers, authors, proof-readers and others accustomed to handling proofs lack confidence in a computer printout as sole evidence of what still has to become 'real' type. They do not see any good reason for having to learn sets of symbols so that the typographic coding can be understood and checked with the design specifications of the finished work; they lack the *visual* information which the galley proof pulled from type gives as to the actual appearance of the text. Unfortunately for the printer it is not often possible to produce convincing arguments which might persuade his customers to accept a printout in place of the familiar 'pull'. Where high-speed photo-typesetting is used a finished proof of the text can be produced quickly in place of the cruder printouts.

There are other factors which the user must recognise. It is not the nature of computer typesetting to offer immediate, calculable cost advantages which can be clearly demonstrated. A computer installation may, indeed, make the difference between a book-printing operation being profitable for the printer or becoming an increasing problem due to wasteful older methods already employed. In this the printer is investing in modern equipment so that he can remain competitive in his chosen markets. But that is not the same as being able to offer a dramatic *saving* as a result of installing new and expensive typesetting equipment. The point emerges as one fundamental to the printing industry's present and future prospects: assuming that the demand for print continues to expand, and that this demand calls, with even more insistence, for stable prices despite the introduction of more expensive methods of conventional production, the leeway for the printer is small: a massive increase in press speeds within the different processes is not immediately likely; the printer's main hope lies in reducing the cost of his *existing* operations and taking short cuts, where he can. Such short cuts are now possible by installing equipment such as that which I have described. The difference, for the customer, may be that he will no longer, with the newer equipment, be able to demand precisely the same facilities as those given him by the old, and may not see an immediate price advantage in the change.

Not only is the ball in the customer's court but it has bounced into the typographer's and designer's courts too. In deciding exactly which of the many different typographical conventions need be incorporated into computer typesetting programs, typographers and others concerned with a printed product's final appearance, have been brought face to face with a need to justify the value of such conventions with more than a recital of aesthetic preferences and prejudices. The question which must now be asked more often, and answered more cogently, is '*Why* do we do it?' The answer may be easy in some cases: we use italics for emphasis, or for visual differentiation which helps the reader better to understand the meaning of the text; capital letters are necessary to improve understanding, and such typographical niceties as even word-spacing, correct word-breaking in justified text and harmonious page make-up all have a practical purpose in aiding text comprehension. For many of these requirements computer typesetting caters with ease. Not all are equally important to every printing job. For other text setting requirements – justified text is the obvious example – the technical problems presented by the latest equipment may be great, and it is desirable that both printers and designers should examine the whole basis of their accepted practice to find out, in essence, whether they are getting value for money from such conventions: whether, in fact, it matters to readers whether all, or only some, of the typographic traditions in printing are retained. What categories of work may dispense with the earlier practices of text composition without detriment? Will readers be prepared for printers to continue making the best use of their less up-to-date machinery and equipment, which may mean that the cost of printing could rise so that the printing industry can remain capable of meeting varying consumer needs?

When considering such problems we are outside the technical context of computer typesetting and in areas in which habit, preference, fashion and other imponderables play roles no less important than hard day-to-day industrial facts of life, and must somehow be equated with them. It may happen that an expanding technology will eventually digest all the vagaries of fashion, variations of typographical approach and design specifications we expect from print. At the moment this is not the case, and it may never become the case unless all concerned are ready to take a new, hard look at what habits we have got into over 400 years of printing. I am not, of course, suggesting that all, or even any, of the existing traditions are valueless, but that their presence should at least be evaluated in relation to their application in specific categories of print. The paperback novel, for example, may need certain standards of legibility and overall typographical design which the scientific paper does not – or vice versa! The fact that both may eventually benefit by modern typesetting methods does, however, call for some knowledge of what the parameters of each are, so that they may be observed in the development, programming and design of the equipment.

11 Bindery: finishing the job

The bindery in a printing works was once, naturally enough, the place where books were bound. Today the bindery may contain equipment other than that used for bookbinding, and the term has been extended to cover that department where a number of operations are carried out on work already printed. All such operations *can* be called 'finishing', but it is a convention of printing terminology to regard 'finishing' as something which is done outside the factory in which the material is printed, while the 'bindery' is more usually a department under the same roof as the presses. The reason for this distinction is probably the persistence of the printer's view of his bindery as a place for bookbinding, even when it has evolved in other directions. I shall nevertheless maintain this distinction, because it marks the difference between what can be called 'in plant' operations and those carried out elsewhere by specialists as a service to the printing industry and which are known as 'trade houses' or 'trade finishers'.

Some printing factories have no bindery at all and use only outside finishing, as and where needed. In some printing groups with several factories the bindery may be located in one of these factories and used as a group service. It is not unusual for printers to send some work to other printers who have the bindery facilities required for particular operations which they cannot carry out themselves. Such work is taken in and charged in exactly the same way as work sent out to a trade finisher, but its availability depends on the spare capacity of the bindery and the business relationship between the two firms.

The great problem of bindery and finishing work is the variety of different sizes, materials and operations required within the wide range of products which general printing encompasses. Even simple items of print, such as a small booklet, require some kind of finishing: the printed sheets have to be cut to size, collated and, perhaps, wire-stapled together to form the booklet. From such relatively easy operations we branch out into a multiplicity of finishing which includes creasing, folding, cutting to special shapes, varnishing, laminating, perforating, insetting and, of course, bookbinding, all of which are, to some degree, necessary so that differing kinds of printed products can be presented in forms which enhance them and suit them better to their various purposes.

When the printer's bindery was solely a place used by craftsmen who bound books by traditional methods its problems were still manageable within the plant. But it took longer to bind a book than to print it, and it was (and still is) common to see a vast number of printed sheets waiting for the bindery to carry out additional work. The trimming, collating, sewing and casemaking which goes on in the traditional bindery is a totally different sort of operation from that required to print a book, and is carried out at different

Hand gold-tooling for a fine binding.

speeds with different equipment and skills. Though the printer is traditionally responsible for binding, craft binding is now a specialised and rare service: the high speeds of modern presses have made it necessary to mechanise most, if not all, of the hand operations which go into making a book and many other such manufactured items of print. Whether hand craft or machines are used, the binding department is, in effect, a separate factory within the print works, and its methods are not easily synchronised with the production of printed matter. Also, binding materials have changed and cannot always be handled in the same ways as those used for traditional bindings.

Most printing plants have a certain amount of bindery equipment, if only a guillotine to trim finished sheets: the printing press does not deliver separate pages in sequence, but pages, or groups of pages, arranged in a system of imposition which requires them to be cut and made available to the bindery for sorting into their correct order (collation). Moreover, a book is not normally made up of a number of separate pages, but is collated in groups of pages called signatures so that it can be bound to open easily at all places and will remain firmly attached to its binding or 'case'. Many of the procedures of craft binding can equally well be carried out automatically in machine binding, and the former does not necessarily produce books which are better bound, though the craft binder's materials and skills are undoubtedly capable of finer finished work than any machine.

The craft gilder's tools. The rabbit's foot is used in manipulating the extremely thin leaves of gold.

The hand work which was done in the bindery has only slowly and gradually been automated, and many hand operations can still be seen in printing plants where the economics of production do not warrant the installation of modern bindery machinery, or where the printed products are of such variety of size and finishing requirements that the standardisation imposed by complete automation is not acceptable or worth the capital which would have to be found for bindery machinery.

The commonest task in the bindery is that of collation, and the most primitive mechanism for this can be found in the 'round table' which is simply a revolving surface with a number of stations at which operatives sit placing pages from piles into sequence as each signature passes in front of them. (A useful distinction which the printer makes might be mentioned here: he regards a 'sheet' as the uncut and untrimmed product of a press as delivered. When the sheet has been cut and folded it becomes a 'signature' which comprises a number of 'pages'.)

Hand-stitching of signatures is still to be found in craft bookbinding.

A rotary adhesive binder.

Machines have been developed which fold, collate, stitch or glue and deliver finished books in a single in-line operation. These are, in effect, moving tracks incorporating ingenious devices for collating signatures and capable of being adjusted within certain size limits to handle different categories of product. At their most advanced such bindery machines can process print almost as rapidly as the printing machines can produce it. An extension of their capabilities is found in the packaging industry, where the mechanisation of carton manufacture – cutting, folding, glueing and other finishing requirements – is carried out in a series of successive in-line operations. More commonly, however, machines designed for specific operations, such as adhesive binding, book forming and pressing, case making, wire stitching, drilling, folding and so on, are kept separate, the better to organise the amount of work which each is required to handle.

It is necessary to remain for a while, for the purposes of clear explanation, with bookbinding while bearing in mind that this is only one of the procedures which may be called for before an item of print can be said to be 'finished'. Enough has already been said to show the nature of the printer's problems in the bindery: he may choose to limit the amount of machinery in this department, but does so at some expense in time and by having to accept that a certain amount of space in his factory will often be occupied unproductively by printed sheets awaiting the attentions of the bindery. If he uses trade bindery services these could increase costs and affect competitive trading. The key is in the length of his printing runs and the degree of standardisation of product he can achieve. A book printer may operate within a wide range of sizes and qualities, but at some stage he has to decide the limits within which he can work efficiently and economically if he wishes to produce a finished job in his own factory. Such standardisation is apparent in the paperback books, which are mass produced to determined formats and materials for a given series. The economics of paperback, or pocket-book, manufacture dictate a much higher degree of standardisation in materials, sizes and production methods for the quantities required and, due to large runs, the printer can more safely install the expensive specialised plant required to handle the bindery work in an automatic line.

A glance along the shelves of any bookshop or library is enough to show the differences in size of case-bound books. Many of these differences are small and are apparently quite arbitrary, in so far as the publisher or designer has decided on a particular size without much concern for the machinery and equipment which will be used in its production. It is true to say that the whole character of a book (and also its price) can be affected by its size. The ability of presses to produce printed sheets of a given size using economical imposition schemes, the trimming of sheets and their subsequent collation, folding and other bindery operations, are all determined by the machinery itself within limits. It might reasonably be asked why case-bound books do not settle down in standard formats, as do most paperbacks, and obtain similar advantages in cost and convenience. To discuss this would mean an examination of the whole subject of standardisation in printing. It is sufficient, for the present, to observe that differences in format – not only for books but for publications, stationery and a whole range of printed material – do exist, and that these variations have a direct bearing on the finishing procedures chosen and often on the printing processes themselves.

Ideally the bindery should be an extension of the mechanical efficiency of the rest of the factory. A certain amount of hand work can be tolerated without losing too much production time, but a flow of printed work into an inefficient bindery is one of the worst bottlenecks a printer has to contend with.

Finishing, in its wider connotation, requires a range of machinery so varied in its design and purposes that merely to list all the finishing operations available would be exhausting. Many finishing tasks are difficult, and many more are made difficult by the fact that the overall design of the print has not taken into consideration the finishing it needs before being put to use. No printer installs *all* the machinery he may need for every kind of finishing. There are hand-operated machines for simple finishing work, such as numbering and eyeletting, and, in a few cases, the printing presses themselves can be adapted to carry out certain operations as part of the printing cycle, though these are more likely to be specialised machines designed for producing particular products, such as business stationery with carbon interleaving, etc. Cutting, folding, insetting and some other operations are done by equipment attached to the presses, in the case of large web-fed installations, for specific categories of print, such as newspapers and journals.

Here a valuable distinction can be made between the wide range of finishing which, at one time or another, print may need and the specialised finishing work which is carried out in a plant devoted to the production of a specific type of product. It is sometimes not realised that 'specialisation' in print is more often specialisation in the ways in which conventionally printed materials are handled *after* presswork than in any special methods used in the preparation and printing of the image. Record sleeves, for example, are basically made by conventional colour preparation and text setting and printing, but the varnish or lamination which protects and enhances the appearance of the print, together with the careful folding and glueing which is needed to make a sleeve of the required size, is, for large-scale production, a matter for specialists with the right machinery and the plant necessary for efficient production and low costs. Here, as in many printing jobs requiring specialised finishing, the advantages of mechanisation are difficult to estimate:

Modern guillotines can make a series of cuts to a pre-set program which controls the movement of side-lays and backstop. The operator feeds and removes the sheets and supervises the cutting sequences.

the printer cannot hope to compete for profitable long-run work unless he has the plant and operational skills available to produce the required goods in quantity and at a competitive price. In the case of a product such as a record sleeve, the costing is extremely fine and, even with the necessary equipment, a fractionally lower cost can persuade big customers to buy the same services and goods elsewhere: the customers themselves are always looking for savings on what is, for them, a closely watched expenditure. In the example we have taken the record companies recognise that, without attractive and even lavish sleeves, their records will not compete for customer-appeal in the shops. On the other hand, the cost of printing and making the sleeves represents an overhead which, if reduced, will yield worthwhile savings in their own total production costs. The printer, therefore, may find that, even with the right plant, he must use every available means for improving the economies of production while maintaining set standards, otherwise he will lose business which is not easily recovered and which, when lost, leaves him with machinery geared to products which can be offered to only a small market.

The brisk competitive climate of printing specialisation has not deterred printers from going for the profitable long-run work which comes from an ability to produce specific products better and quicker than the general commercial printer, whose plant is geared to diversity rather than specialisation. With record sleeves we are on the borders of a completely different sector of the industry – packaging and paper converting – which, as the names imply, are more concerned with what is done *to* print than with printing itself. The printing of cartons, for example, is only the first, and by no means the most difficult, stage in the production of the finished, three-dimensional product, folded and glued. Paper converting and packaging are outside the scope of this book, but provide an interesting example of just how important the finishing processes can be: important enough to grow into a new industry in its own right.

As I have said, the general printer is ready, from time to time, to use finishing services for any operation which he cannot carry out in his own works. These services are bought by the printer, and their cost is charged to the eventual buyer as part of the printing job itself. This can be expensive, since the trade finisher's profit is added to the printer's profit in the final price, which may incorporate not only the finishing work itself but also the handling and transportation of the print between the printer's and the finisher's factories. The skilled buying of print has to take into account the relative merits of using a particular printer because he happens to have the equipment needed to complete a job, and the placing of work with printers who may be more suited to the work in hand so far as the printing goes, but will have to send out the job for specialist finishing. Much depends on what finishing is indicated in the original design, and a great deal can be achieved by the designer who 'tailors' his concept to the resources which are available for its completion.

The question, at this stage, is whether the finishing specified is correctly related to the purpose of the printed job, or in some other way adds to its effectiveness. Sometimes it obviously does. Take, as an example, the tickets which are printed to hang inside a garment to be sold in a multiple store. Many hundreds of thousands of tickets may be ordered, and after printing a hole needs to be punched in each and string inserted so that the tickets can be attached to the garments. To do this by hand would be tedious and expensive in time and labour. Machines exist which will punch and string such tickets automatically, at high speeds, and trade finishers who install these machines can offer this finishing operation as a trade service to printers. The tickets would be of little use without some means of attaching them where they are needed, and this item of trade finishing is undoubtedly part of what is required before the job is ready for delivery.

A large number of bindery and trade finishing operations fall into this category. To mention but a few, the numbering of tickets or documents in sequence, the rounding of corners on formal cards such as invitations, wedding announcements, etc, edge-gilding, scoring, perforating, eyeletting and spiral binding. Beyond these finishing operations, which have to do with the uses to which print is put, come a number of finishing tasks which are meant to enhance the appearance of the print. The dividing line between 'utility' finishing and decorative or 'aesthetic' finishing is imprecise. The application of certain transparent varnishes or film laminates can impart a surface glamour to print, and are often used to this end entirely. On the other hand, surface varnishes and transparent laminates protect the print underneath by sealing it away from dirt. A piece of printing may therefore be laminated for good reasons (an instruction booklet, which may be handled near oily machinery, requires such protection if it is to have a usefully long life). But quite a lot of surface treatment, special bindings and other finishes are used to give prestige and the appearance of luxury to a job.

Incidentally, with particular reference to varnishing and laminating, the decision to carry out these finishing operations should be taken at the inception of a design, not as an afterthought: the application of varnishes and laminates can affect the behaviour of the inks they cover and, with some colours, special formulations may be needed before a varnish or laminate can successfully be applied over the printed page.

Print which is intended for display usually needs to be folded, cut and manipulated in various ways so that it can do its job properly. Counter displays may be free-standing and made of heavy-gauge materials which are either printed or with which print is incorporated. Again we are close to the allied industries of packaging and display rather than the world of 'pure' print. General printers may have to call on trade houses for finishing, and are rarely geared for large and continuing contracts involving specialist finishing machinery other than the bindery equipment which they have decided to install. The construction of the cutting and creasing dies used in producing special shapes and folds is a difficult and skilled task, and most of this work has been cornered by factories specially equipped for it. There remains, as I have already said, quite a large quantity of 'one-off' jobs which call for the finisher's techniques and machines. Once again one is bound to say that a proportion of it is less successful than it should be due to lack of forethought at the design stage. A well-known firm of London trade finishers tells me that much of their time

A typical folding machine in a bindery.

and effort is dedicated to 'rescuing' jobs which have been printed in ways which compli-
cate or hinder the work which has to be done to finish them. Printers and designers
themselves are not always as knowledgeable as they should be about finishing requirements and commence the printing without consultation with the experts whose part of the
responsibility for the final product is implied. But, as always, the printer's influence over
the *origination* of print design is only partial or, in some cases, non-existent, and decisions
are often taken before he comes into the picture, which limits his ability to print prudently
and with a view to later procedures.

Generally, anything which needs to be done to print is done after the presses have
completed their part of the job. Some reference should be made to the commest finishing
machine to be found in a printing works – the guillotine, or cutter. This is a large knife
which slices up print into required sizes and, for the greater part of its history, this is
about all that could be said of its function in the print factory. Apart from safety factors,
and the maintenance of accurate cutting, guillotining has always been a mechanical
operation requiring only the setting of 'lays' (the back and side stops which determine the
positioning of the paper pile under the knife). Today's guillotines are more complex, and
the most modern are capable of being programmed to carry out pre-set cutting sequences
automatically; that is without adjustment by the operator. The cutting program is 'read in'
to the machine and is, in effect, registered as a series of impulses on a magnetic tape which,
in turn, electrically operates the mechanism which makes the necessary mechanical settings for a determined series of cuts. Such guillotines may have a number of separate
channels, each of which is capable of accepting a cutting program, so the operator with

jobs which require cutting in varying dimensions, laterally and longitudinally, has only to select the program for the initial cut for the machine to make a series of precise and predetermined cuts and, for the second series of cuts, bring in a second program which dictates cuts to different dimensions.

Programmed guillotines have appreciably speeded – and made more accurate – the cutting of printed sheets, which must always, to some degree, be a potential bottleneck between press and bindery. All guillotines are capable of making only one cut at a time. There are other paper-cutting machines which will, by using three or four knives, cut (or, in this case, trim) a pile of paper on three or four sides in one operation, though it has not been necessary to make programs available for these, since such trimming is always carried out to a fixed size for a particular job.

Another machine which can conveniently be considered in our present category is not a finishing machine at all, since it is used as part of printing-plate preparation. This is the step and repeat machine, the name of which gives a good clue to its function. Some printing jobs require the replication of large numbers of relatively small identical motifs – labels, for example – which it would obviously be wasteful to print individually. Such print is best produced by printing with large plates containing a number of identical images, the items being cut from the sheet after printing. The step and repeat machine is an ingenious piece of equipment which produces photographic negatives with many images of the same subject. The lateral and horizontal movement of the photographic head is controlled so that, from an original, a number of identical photographic images is made. These may be projected directly on to an offset printing plate which, when developed, will carry the required number of 'copies' for printing, *en masse*.

To complete this brief exploration of bindery and finishing we return to the bindery itself in its traditional role. The making of a case-bound book involves so many separate operations that it is hard to see how it can be automated to the same advanced degree as typesetting and printing. To examine only one detail, the books (of various sizes, of course) are sewn, and the backs rounded. The craftsman bookbinder does the latter work by clamping the book in a vice and literally hammering it into the desired shape. If adhesive is applied to the spine so that the outer cover will stick it is desirable to roughen the surface to which the spine is glued so that the spine sticks evenly and well. Here again the most reliable way is to use human hands and judgement.

In fact, machinery has been made which will carry out these and other operations and produce books which, on cursory examination at least, are indistinguishable from hand craftsmanship. For the many books and journals which are now printed in large numbers and at low price for a voracious consumer market some method had to be found which would both speed and cheapen the method of covering them. Paperbacks and magazines do not have heavy board covers, so the problem was modified by having to apply only a comparatively light weight of cover board, or even paper or plastic. Adhesive binding suggested an immediate and possible answer. In practice, though, the task of sticking covers to books is not as easy as it seems at first. It is not enough that the cover adheres to the spine and provides a protection for the pages: the cover becomes *part* of the book, and is put under some strain when the book is opened and the pages turned. The collation of pages in signatures is no longer possible when adhesives are used, since, without sewing, the signature does not hold all the pages in contact with the spine. Books bound by adhesive are, in effect, 'loose leaf' books, trimmed on all four sides. Adhesives which will hold each separate page in place, bear a certain amount of strain and still maintain the page's tiny purchase on the spine are by no means easy to find. A book should have a reasonably long life, and may be exposed to extremes of temperature and humidity in some countries which it would not normally encounter in temperate latitudes. The adhesive must therefore not only be able to stick; it must remain firm over the useful life of the book, so that it can be opened and closed, and remain flexible without the adhesive drying out and becoming brittle. But, in production, the adhesive must dry quickly and positively enough for the high speed at which the books are bound.

Anyone with experience of adhesive binding will know that some books have been bound by this method which do not stand up to normal usage, and which deteriorate after quite short periods and shed pages, or detach themselves from the covers altogether. The persistence with which the paperback printers and publishers have pursued the goal of adhesive binding is evidence of their desire to perfect a means of binding large numbers of books by machine. Given the right adhesive, it is no great mechanical problem to apply it, place the cover in position and produce the finished book as an in-line operation at speed. The problem is durability and the capacity to withstand the strains of normal use.

With journals and magazines the problems are not so critical: these are usually less bulky, and have a shorter useful life than a book, though adhesives do not always behave well when applied to art papers such as are used in much magazine printing. There are advantages to the reader: adhesive-bound books open flat and can be neatly squared at the spine.

Various methods have been used to overcome the difficulties of adhesive binding. The roughening or cutting of the spine to obtain better grip is common as part of machine binding technique, and fabrics are sometimes used to reinforce the spine and take the adhesive before the covers are applied. Adhesive binding can be used for hard-covered books, where the problems remain much the same as for paperbacks. Large runs of hard-back books, such as those produced for the *Reader's Digest* book clubs, are adhesive bound, rounded and backed and cased-in as a continuous operation.

12 Paper and ink

Paper and ink are often called the printer's 'raw materials'. In the sense that they are both essential to printing, the term is acceptable, but neither is, strictly speaking, a 'raw material', since each is manufactured, and in a great variety of different substances or formulations. In a finished piece of print, ink and paper are indivisibly bound – the two together are, in fact, all that can be called 'print' in the material sense. It is strange, therefore, that so little attention is paid by users to the behaviour and characteristics of these elements. Paper is certainly a large item in the cost of printing: it is bought by the customer and, however much he may imagine that he is buying something called 'print', he is certainly paying up to the hilt for paper and ink.

Papermaking is an ancient craft, and one not easy to understand. As papermakers never tire of pointing out, paper is not a stable manufactured substance so much as a natural product which has been processed. One basic ingredient of good paper is wood pulp, and in some mills abroad it is possible to see tree-trunks being fed into the plant for pulping, the pulp being processed and the paper issuing from the machines at the other end of the mill. The point which the papermakers, in their own interests, want to get home is that, with organic raw materials, however carefully and skilfully the manufacturing process is controlled, variations in the consistency of the end product are inevitable. During its journey from pulp to paper the 'mix', from which the papermaking machines produce a sheet of the required thickness (substance) and surface, will take in added ingredients, mostly chemicals, all of which are intended to impart particular qualities to the paper and improve its value to the user for printing for various purposes and by differing processes.

At its simplest papermaking is the addition of water to wood pulp, which is then passed through machines which progressively extract the water and dry the moving 'web' of paper, at the same time causing the separate fibres in the pulp to unite, giving strength to the paper. The length of a papermaking machine is some indication of the adjustments which have to be made along the way if the wet mixture is to be processed to obtain a predictable weight and quality of paper at the 'dry end'. The paper may then be used as a base for further treatment, including coating with mixtures which give it (either on one side or both) a particularly high surface gloss and density.

Wood is not the only substance used in papermaking. Indeed, almost any substance with a fibrous quality capable of pulping will make a paper of some sort or another, and commercial papermaking utilises esparto grass, waste paper and rags in obtaining a mix suitable for various grades of finished paper. The whole papermaking process is so intriguing and mysterious that it becomes a subject in itself, worthy of careful study. For my present purposes, however, I shall resist too detailed an exploration of papermaking itself and examine the characteristics of paper as encountered in printing. It is nevertheless necessary to keep in mind the conditions which govern its production, if only to understand what can happen in the various stages between leaving the mill and reaching the reader in the form of a printed product, such as a book or newspaper.

It is relevant that commercial papermaking methods are not suited to small-scale production. In spite of the immense variety of branded products, the papermakers are committed to large-scale makings and must carefully anticipate the market for a particular paper or accept the consequences of having produced large quantities of something which will not sell. At one time in Britain there were a number of smaller mills prepared to undertake special makings to the specifications of a customer. Nowadays commercial papermaking is almost entirely for the big groups capable of making vast investments in machinery and materials. Like the food in the packets at a supermarket, papers are attractively presented but often without very much information on what goes into them. This is partly because the printing industry has frequently regarded paper simply as a raw product to be purchased at a given price and has taken little or no interest in its manufacture. Certain papers are categorised as 'wood free' or 'rag', 'machine coated' or

A raw material of paper, wood pulp, is stacked to await pulping.

Stock flowing on to the 'wet end' of a paper machine.

'brush coated', but it is the exception to find a printer fully equipped accurately to assess the quality and characteristics of all grades and finishes under printing conditions, or in possession of testing equipment for exact measurement of a paper's printability. More often the printer – like the housewife at the supermarket – buys the product with which he is most familiar and which, from experience, he thinks will meet the consumer's needs without likelihood of trouble and complaint along the way.

The result of this rather slap-happy relationship between papermaker and printer has not always been for the good of either. On the papermaker's side he is constantly being urged to provide papers with particular characteristics – greater whiteness, opacity or surface smoothness – with little concern, on his customer's part, as to how he obtains, and maintains, these qualities throughout large-scale production. The number of additives to the basic mix has increased commensurately with the increase in the number of different purposes to which paper and, of course, board (the heavier weights) are put. A mention of some of the characteristics which a printer may ask for in his papers will give an idea of the range of qualities which must somehow be obtained by adding water to fibres and taking it out again.

Substance and finish

The substance of a paper is commonly taken to be its thickness. The heavier a paper (papers are sold by weight), the more likely it is to remain opaque to print. Weight is not always a gauge of quality (as is obvious with the heavier kraft or wrapping papers, which are thick but of low quality due to the cheap base ingredients). The paper may be regulated by the machine to any reasonable thickness. The weight of the paper has some bearing on its printability, though surface quality is probably more important in this area. Paper is compressible and, because the printing processes (particularly the letterpress process) involve pressure, the heavier papers are less likely to suffer from the stresses of printing. Heavier printing papers work out more expensive per pound and, of course, their bulk is a factor in deciding their suitability for the finished print: a book in heavy paper is bulkier and may be more difficult to cut, fold and bind; and, beyond a certain weight, the reader is made uncomfortably aware of the paper's heaviness.

Paper should be opaque if it is to be printed both sides, otherwise the image will show through and disturb the clarity of what is printed on the reverse side. Weight and opacity are linked in so far as one helps the other: a heavier paper will normally be more opaque than a lighter one. But, due to the considerations already mentioned (primarily cost), the aim is normally to obtain the greatest degree of opacity in the weight required, even if this is a lightweight paper. This is where chemistry comes into papermaking. The opacity of paper can be affected in many ways, either by additives at the mixing stage or, more usually, by coatings applied to the paper during or after manufacture. These coated papers (often loosely called 'art papers') are made in many different ways, the method of applying the coating being critical in the assessment of the printability of the finished surface. The body paper used for coating is usually made of esparto grass, and the coating itself (applied by rollers and brushes) is prepared from a mixture of *blanc fixe*, china clay and a binding agent, usually casein. The purpose of the coating is to fill up any unevenness in the base paper and present a smoother surface to the printing medium. The surface of a coated paper does not have to be glossy, but it usually is, the added reflectance of a gloss coating being a further aid to opacity, due to the paper's greater ability to reflect light from its surface.

Coated paper has, in recent years, been made on machines which, in effect, skim the coating with a blade after the making of the base paper so that it is applied to a determined thickness. This has enabled papermakers with blade-coating machines to produce coated papers at higher speeds, and therefore more cheaply, than the more delicate procedure of brush-coating. The coatings thus applied have been considered less reliable compared with traditional coating methods, but papermakers have improved blade-coating techniques to a point at which satisfactory results can be obtained consistently in the cheaper grades. One of the effects has been to make coated papers available for many jobs which, due to the quantities of paper required, could not otherwise have been economically printed on coated stock. The evenness of the surface imparted by paper coatings enables colour printing to be carried out effectively, and blade coated papers have opened up the possibilities of colour for a number of journals which would otherwise have considered the colour quality obtained on uncoated papers unacceptable.

Surface finish need not be a matter of coating: calendering is a basic finish which papermakers can apply to paper on the web. The paper thus made is said to be 'machine

The 'dry end' of a papermaking machine.

finished' if it receives no further treatment than that which it gets by passing through the calendering rollers in the papermaking machine. Calendering (or 'super-calendering' to distinguish it from the calendering the paper receives from rollers in normal production) is a further processing of the paper by passing it through chilled rollers alternating with rollers made of compressed cotton or paper which compress its surface, giving a harder surface and a higher finish. Paper may be 'polished' after making, or, as 'imitation art', given a thin film of warm water on its underside when passing through the papermaking machine so that the mineral content of the mix is brought to the surface before passing through the calendering rollers of the machine. All these techniques are used to produce differing surface characteristics, but it must be emphasised that each must be selected for a particular making.

Coloured pulps are used for coloured papers, and an important additive at the finishing stage may be a size which improves the hardness of the paper. Size is normally added during the mixing of the pulp before paper is made.

These and many other techniques are concerned entirely with fitting the paper for the variety of uses to which it will be put. Leaving aside special papers, such as label papers, carbon papers and other products designed for special uses, the range of printing papers is vast and there is considerable duplication of grades and prices within categories. The printer buys his paper with an eye to cost and appearance, and in the hope that it will respond well to the printing skills which will be used to transform this 'raw material' into printed work.

A number of things can happen to paper after it is made which affect its printability to a greater or lesser degree. Paper is hygroscopic – it takes water from the atmosphere – and this can obviously affect its composition and, hence, its behaviour in printing. Serious temperature variations will cause paper to shrink and assume a wavy appearance in the pile. In printing it is important for the paper to lie flat and behave well in the machine, not only because the accuracy of the printed impression depends on the accuracy with which the paper can be placed in contact with the printing unit but also because, before this happens, the sheet passes through a mechanical feed for transport to the printing surface. Properly adjusted, the feed mechanism of the press should handle sheet after sheet of paper

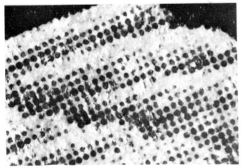

Lithography can be used on relatively rough paper surfaces, but this surface roughness has an effect on the image produced. These illustrations show an investigation of the fall-off in tonal quality between two different paper surfaces. Inferior dot reproduction occurs in relation to the rougher paper surface illustrated above.

of like size, bringing each into the correct position for printing accurately. If the paper has, in any way, departed from its flatness or shrunk and altered its dimensions printing, particularly when over-printing more than one colour, can become a very wearisome business; second, third or fourth printings are hard to hold in exact register and – perhaps even more important to the printer's productivity – the misfeeding of paper can bring about wastage both in materials and time and labour due to having to stop and restart the press because of misfeeds.

As we have seen in our discussion of the offset process, this method of printing depends on an extremely critical balance between water and ink, which is obtained by careful settings of press controls. The condition of the paper itself has, at the moment of accepting an

Printed paper can be put to many uses. These dresses are made from paper.

offset impression, a part to play in this balance. The offset printer is consequently as sensitive to the condition of his paper as he is to the ambient atmosphere of his press room.

The factors so far discussed are all ones which bother the printer more than his customers; the latter pay for a completed job and judge their print on cost and results. To obtain the results it is sensible, on the printer's part, to foresee things which could lead to waste or to production hold-ups, otherwise his profit can be swallowed in production losses caused by stoppages on his machines. This accounts for the somewhat delicate relationship between papermakers and printers. On the one hand, the papermaker looks to the printer, his customer, to discover how he may serve him and supply what is best and most economical for profitable printing which will also please the printer's customers. On the other, the printer's dependence on the papermaker is uncomfortable: if, due to paper deficiencies, he spoils a job he may have to delay delivery so that the work can be done properly. But his customer, who thinks of himself as dealing with a printer, is unlikely to be sympathetic if the blame is put elsewhere: all he knows is that the *printer* has failed him, either in quality or delivery, and complaints about paper are inclined to sound academic on such occasions.

In practice, the skills of papermakers are such that a remarkable degree of consistency, quality and variety is available to those who choose carefully. Few people really know exactly what they mean by 'a good paper', but few are not pleasantly aware of paper quality when they handle work which has been printed on papers well suited to the job.

More can happen to spoil a paper after it has left the papermaking machine than ever happens in the manufacturing process itself. The things which can happen to paper before, during and after printing range from damage due to mishandling to attack by insects. The most frequent paper problem encountered by printers is distortion caused by temperature changes when, for example, paper is taken from storage in a warehouse where it is cool or cold into the relative warmth of the press room. This can cause shrinkage in the paper as it gives up moisture to the warmer atmosphere. The difficulty can be solved either by air conditioning, which equalises temperature and humidity throughout the factory, or by storing paper to be used for printing in the press room for a period before it is used, thus allowing it to adjust to the temperature difference. Dimensional changes in paper can also take place during the actual printing where paper is taken from the reel into a press with a number of separate colour units. Such a press uses rapid drying after each colour is printed. Drying is normally carried out by heat applied directly to the web as it passes from one printing unit to another. This heat can materially affect register due to the moisture extracted, which can cause changes in the dimensions of the paper.

The expansion of web-printing from reels of paper, as contrasted with sheets fed from a pile, has brought to the fore a number of paper problems associated with this method of printing. One is the need for extremely good reeling on the part of the manufacturer, so that the paper comes off the reel and is fed into the press accurately. There are also stresses at work during printing which can distort paper. Paper going through a web-fed offset press or rotary letterpress machine is under considerable tension and is travelling at a very high speed – thousands of feet per minute – but it must, in multi-colour printing, pass through the printing units on the press so that their successive impressions fall, again and again, in exact register. The storage of reels on their sides can, due to the weight of the paper, cause distortion in the reel itself, which is visible as an alarming wobble when the reel is on the working press, and which causes a variable tension on the web as it is fed into the press.

Another paper hazard is encountered when high-speed presses which incorporate cutters and folders are used. This is the paper dust which hangs in the air as fine particles. Dust is a nuisance to the printer, particularly when it settles on the surface of plates and is transferred to the printed image as spots and flecks. The control of dust in a printing plant

Ink additives are carefully weighed before being incorporated with the pigments and other chemicals needed for many different kinds of ink formulation.

(together with the control of ink mist – a fine suspension of ink particles which occurs on and around presses running at very high speeds) is, like air conditioning, a matter of installing the right equipment to deal with the problem. All this is a reminder of the considerable investment in capital equipment, other than printing machinery, which a modern printing plant may face when entering the field of high-speed printing.

Inks are, at first sight, a more bewildering subject even than paper: their colours, formulations and appearance on the finished print exist in innumerable combinations and permutations and, without scientific tests and a knowledge of chemistry, it is virtually impossible to understand exactly how an ink will behave and what it will, or will not, do in the press and on the paper. Inkmaking is a technically advanced industry and, unlike papermaking, it is possible to experiment with different formulations in relatively small quantities and to control results during manufacture more exactly. An adjustment can be made to the content of an ink which will materially assist its performance in a given process or for a special effect. In the past printing inks have been made (and often made by the printers who use them) out of a variety of homely materials. In modern times inkmaking has passed from the print shop into the laboratories and factories of the suppliers, and the inks now have branded names and specified qualities and characteristics.

Ink must, however, be transferred to that much more temperamental surface, paper, and, often, to other surfaces, such as plastic film, metal or absorbent board. Were it not for the unpredictability and variety of printable surfaces, it would no doubt by now have been possible to provide a series of ink formulations suited to the majority of jobs. But an ink transferred by a press to paper always has about it an element of unpredictability as to its final appearance. Leaving aside 'special' inks (such as bronze, gold or silver), printing inks are all composed of a base – oil or water is common – and a pigment in suspension. To this may be added other chemicals which, in different ways, affect behaviour during printing.

When printing presses were operated by hand, or were slow 'automatics' compared with today's high-speed units, the main problem was to obtain a good black impression which would not smudge and which would retain its colour and covering ability. The success of these matchings of ink and paper can be appreciated by examining printed work of earlier times, much of which, in blackness and crispness of impression and lack of discoloration in either ink or paper, is a tribute to the quality of materials and the craftsmanship employed in their making and their use by the printer. Today print may be more ephemeral: nobody cares whether an admission ticket survives after the function for which it has been printed; today's newspaper is replaced by tomorrow's; the cheaper paperback is not designed to be kept for a long time. Print may be bought for a variety of reasons, one of them being (as with the newspaper) for immediate consumption. Inks and papers, therefore, are designed for various purposes and, being varied, the materials themselves are specifically adjusted to the requirements of the end product.

Inks, then, not only conform to the demands of the process in which they are used but help the printer make the best he can of a variety of jobs carried out by that process. When printers had only single-colour printing by the letterpress process to think about ink-making could well be made part of the printing work itself. Sheet-fed letterpress inks are usually oil-based and contain fewer solvents than inks used for the very high-speed printing processes. Inks must be matched in formulation to the type of surface on to which the printing machine will impress them. And, of course, inkmaking is at the centre of the whole mystique of colour printing. I have observed elsewhere how difficult it seems to be for people to recognise that what they see reproduced in print is, in fact, the colours (and colour mixtures) achieved by *printing* inks which are different in formulation and method of application from the oil or water-colour pigments of painters and the dyes used in making photographic colour transparencies. The technical side of colour printing is dealt with in the chapter on illustration, but it is appropriate to say that a large part of the *craft* in print today lies in the combined knowledge, experience and skill of papermaker, inkmaker and printer working together to achieve the greatest possible fidelity to original work in other media.

The ink film on a piece of print is usually extremely thin, varying between 0·1 and 0·5 thousandths of an inch. Offset films are thinnest, and the thickest are those laid down by screen process. Pigments used in printing inks are ground extremely finely (0–25 microns). The thin film must meet with many demands other than that of laying down colour: it must dry quickly, it may have to possess durability and be weatherproof for outdoor use, it may need a gloss or matt finish and it must be suited not only to the printing process but also to the paper used for a particular job. To incorporate these qualities in a substance which is so sparingly applied is a meticulous task and one which presents problems which inkmakers never finally solve, since printing machinery and papers are themselves always changing and developing in ways which affect the inks used.

13 What happens next?

It would be easier to write about the future of printing were it possible to say that present developments in the industry had been fully assimilated. Another factor inhibiting ready prediction is uncertainty as to whether the printer's customers, the users and consumers of print, will adapt readily and fully to the changes which could be brought about by new equipment and methods. The completely up-to-date printing plant, in terms of machines and equipment, does not exist; rather do we find that specific areas of production are tackled in accordance with the demands of particular print categories. Thus we may find advanced typesetting systems working in conjunction with conventional plant in the machine room, or highly developed machines being served by out-dated methods of composition. This is not caused entirely by an unwillingness on the printer's part to embrace newer and better ways of doing the job. It is partly due to the fact that 'the job' imposes its own limits on the ease with which modern equipment can be introduced profitably, and partly the need to cater for varying print designs and specifications. The printing industry does not abandon a piece of useful equipment simply because manufacturers offer an apparently more efficient or economical way of doing a particular job in the printing sequence, and enough has already been said to show why: all the printer's equipment is related in its functions, and the desirability of installing new systems must be judged on a number of conditions which may have little immediately to do with the efficiency, or otherwise, of a particular development.

The reader may, by now, be getting a little impatient at my insistence on the customer's responsibility in adjusting to changed methods of production and be wondering whether printers themselves do not wait too long, and need too much reassurance, in breaking with traditional methods. This may sometimes be so, but it is also true to say that the degree of standardisation imposed by faster, cheaper printing techniques has often proved hard to sell to customers, in spite of price, or other, advantages it brings.

It must also be remembered that the basic principles underlying the three main printing processes have not changed in spite of impressive progress in pre-press procedures and, in my view, are unlikely to show any fundamental departure from the norms in the foreseeable future.

With these provisos it is still possible to say with some confidence that changes will come and that many of these changes will materially affect the ways in which we make and use print. After many centuries of isolation from industrial change, printing has now learned how to adapt, for its own purposes, developments in other industries. Progress in optics, chemistry, plastics, electronics, fluidics and other spheres of technology have contributed effectively to printing progress, and the speed with which such possibilities, when presented from outside the industry, are realised in printing terms has greatly increased. The continuing development of printing, therefore, is likely for some time to be the continuing absorption by the industry of those changes, technical and operational, which already impinge. This may seem a somewhat undramatic view of printing's future; we are less impressed, these days, by steady progress than by the spectacular breakthrough. Yet it is true that presses now print faster and more accurately on a wider range of materials than they could even a few years ago; printing plates for letterpress and offset are in an advanced state of development; computers and other equipment have offered the possibility of extremely swift and economical ways of setting, storing and updating matter for printing; new communications methods have freed the printing plant from a strict mechanical and operational interdependence between departments; and so on.

Before discussing technical possibilities it is necessary to make some reference to another factor which affects the rate of progress of printing – the management–labour structure of the industry. This has not always shown itself capable of withstanding the stresses of adjustment to new materials, machines and methods, and a great deal of time and effort have been devoted to trying to find out why this kind of problem arises and how it can be solved. One view of the future is that printing will make its final spurt into the twentieth century only when management abandons many of its present preoccupations and preconceptions, and the labour force is educated to a more responsive and responsible attitude to technical progress. This, in a nutshell, is what a great deal of the advice which the industry has been getting, officially and unofficially, in recent years comes down to. But a diagnosis is not a cure, and little really constructive has been said which can apply uniformly to the whole industry. Smaller firms have long been woefully undercapitalised and, thereby, prevented from taking advantage of plant improvements which would have allowed them to compete more effectively in their chosen markets. It seems probable that only the very small printer – the jobbing shop catering for local needs – will escape the need to amalgamate or be taken over by a bigger group if full advantage is to be taken of new methods. These are more often designed for the larger group, where optimum productivity is of paramount importance. Already these larger groupings, with a number of factories and services operating to a centralised administration, have taken the place of the former pattern of large and small printers, each ploughing his own furrow and competing on personal service.

On the other hand, the smaller, independent firm is now offered (provided it can find the money and skilled labour needed) tempting possibilities which, if properly costed and evaluated, can place it almost overnight into a strongly competitive position *vis-à-vis* the large printing groups. A single item of high-production plant, correctly used, good costing and specialisation in an expanding category of print can promote what was formerly a small plant capable of only limited productivity into the big league and ahead of even its most powerful competitors: printing is not exempt from the industrial imperatives which dictate that success comes from the right job being done at the right price.

Of the printing trade unions it need only be said that the future patterns have already been defined and, if they are followed, should ease the labour force into the modern context with the minimum of fuss. The strict craft divisions which characterised earlier printing methods gave rise to a large number of unions, each concerned with the welfare of its membership inside departmental lines. Such compartmentalisation has been blurred, or completely destroyed, by the very nature of much of the newer equipment in use for printing. For example, compositors formerly working entirely with metal type may now be required to retrain for computer-aided composition, where keyboarding and the handling of film takes the place of the earlier craft training in hot-metal composition. The preparation of a photo-polymer plate for a letterpress machine has much in common, in skills needed and equipment used, with the production of an offset plate. In these, and many other, instances we experience the crumbling of craft divisions, and the unions have had to adapt to this merging and changing of responsibilities. The classic 'who does what' dispute is still being fought out in printing, but union amalgamations have contributed much to a more realistic attitude to demarcation and the needs of new methods, as well as reducing that other source of industrial tension, inter-union rivalry. The future, it has been predicted by union leaders and printing managements alike, will bring even closer associations and merging between printing unions, with a consequent advantage to all concerned in negotiations. A single printing union could be as powerful an instrument of technical progress as the industry has had in the whole of its history. With it could come improved training methods and the abandonment of entrenched ideas on the way in which jobs are done.

Some of the more spectacular possibilities for the future lie outside the actual printing plant and within the developing field of communications. Given the increasing versatility and availability of new composing and other pre-press operations, the decentralisation made possible by the transmission of text and illustration from remote terminals to a central printing plant, which comprises only presses, has attractive advantages for printer and customer alike. Newspapers in Britain, America, Sweden, Japan and elsewhere are already using facsimile transmission equipment to send complete pages by radio or telephone cable link (and in Russia by satellite link) *from* a central publishing house *to* distant centres for printing. Here, it would seem, the position of the commercial printer is reversed, and the outlying areas carry out the printing while the central office transmits the prepared pages. For commercial purposes it is more likely that the advantages of outlying stations for the processing of copy up to press stage will be sought, so that the printing plant itself can be centrally developed to an advanced stage of efficiency and versatility to deal with incoming material arriving (probably as a display on a cathode-ray tube) from outlying 'stations' and from which printing plates can immediately be made.

The computer's ability to handle 'raw' copy and incorporate typographical and format requirements has already been extended to systems which provide a visual display from computer storage. This can be presented, line-by-line, to sensitised paper or film to provide an immediately usable paper or film image for platemaking. This completely eliminates the need for the intervening use of a photo-typesetting machine to handle the computer's output and transform it into film. No doubt whole pages will soon be computer-generated and transmitted from computer typesetting centres to printing plants, where the received images will be used for the direct creation of printing plates. Such transmitted material may also be stored, on reception, on magnetic tapes for scheduled use when platemaking is convenient.

This arrangement allows one to envisage the setting up of offices where the printer's customers can supervise the processing of their orders, obtain proofs, carry out corrections and deal, in every sense, directly with the printer, without the need to be in contact with the actual production plant. The use of high-speed typesetting systems to serve the composing needs of several production plants would overcome the perennial problem of correlating the speed of composition with the production speed of the presses.

In any event, it is difficult to foresee the indefinite perpetuation of the composing room, as it is now used, as an essential part of a printing plant. Massive computer storage of types, and computer processing to typographical and format requirements, seem to show a clear path to the ultimate use of centralised composition 'banks' to which printers, either as associated companies within a printing and publishing group or as individual sub-scribers, can literally 'dial' for a required quantity of setting and illustration, colour separation and other preparation stages and receive all that is needed to start printing. Already a printer can operate keyboards the output of which is sent for computer-aided typesetting at a central point which returns film. Such a dispersal of the printer's traditional in-plant operations may take some time, even after the technical means have been developed: printers do not willingly cede direct control over the details of their preparation stages to standardised, remotely operated centres and will need substantial reassurance that, if they do, the needs of their customers will be fully met by such systems.

Also in the area of translating originals into print, current developments in Optical Character Recognition (OCR) look promising. Few of the present composing systems will handle setting without the need for keyboarding at some stage, and none will give the complete range of style, content and format demanded for all printing needs. The *origination* of input into whatever new equipment is used has been a preoccupation of development workers in printing for as long as the high-speed systems have been with us. OCR utilises the ability of certain equipment to 'recognise' written characters and translate them into signals which will activate the typesetting system and produce setting from scanned copy. OCR is, then, an automation of the operator 'reading' which is necessary for the manual keyboarding needed by most typesetting systems. This elimination, at input stage, of the human element indicates a possibility of obtaining extremely high speeds and materially shortening the distance between 'raw' copy and composed text.

The initial objection to OCR was that it required the creation of special characters for the recognition equipment to differentiate between one and another. This brought the thing back to square one with a keyboarding requirement no less demanding than ordinary setting and, therefore, of no special advantage at the input stage. OCR has, however, been under active development in conjunction with advanced typesetting systems, and there is reason to hope for equipment which will correctly interpret an original text, typewritten or even handwritten, together with any corrections and stylistic peculiarities, and supply reliable input to a photo-typesetting and formatting system. Existing material which has been typeset and is required for resetting and reprinting is already comparatively easily handled by OCR and, of course, we have a simple form of machine recognition at work in the present systems used for the automatic sorting of documents by equipment which senses the differences between specially designed figures, such as those found on most cheques.

This and other developments are, it will be seen, all aimed at a simplification and a standardisation of the procedures by which material to be printed can be presented to the presses in the forms required by the different processes. The future of such developments as those so far mentioned will depend, to a large extent, on the printing industry's capability of incorporating them into those other parts of its production sequences which remain materially unchanged. At present all presses need a printing surface, and it is what can be got, with the minimum of wasted effort, on to that surface which largely determines the profitability of the plant. Clearly, advanced typesetting systems are of real value only when the throughput of text is high. Many printers (such as those producing colour printing for packaging) can afford to ignore the search for highly automated text composing methods without necessarily being reactionary or unprogressive.

So far I have referred to nothing which offers the likelihood of a changed method of printing. Among the main and subsidiary processes described in earlier chapters enough will have been gleaned of their individual requirements to see that, unless they remain for a long time as main printing processes, there is not much point in discussing print as we know it at all. There is, nevertheless, an existing method of obtaining a replicated image which has been the subject of considerable interest on the development side of print, particularly in the United States. This is electrostatic printing. The electrostatic principle is used successfully, and at quite high speeds, by a range of document-copying equipment employing xerography.

In xerographic copying the surface of a coated plate (or drum) is sensitised by an electrically charged grid which moves across it. The coating of the plate is now charged with positive electricity. The original of which a copy is to be made is projected on to the coated plate. Positive electrical charges disappear in the areas exposed to light. A *negatively* charged powder is dusted over the plate and adheres to the *positively* charged image. Paper is placed over the plate and receives a positive charge, which enables it to attract the image-forming powder from the plate, forming a positive image. The print is

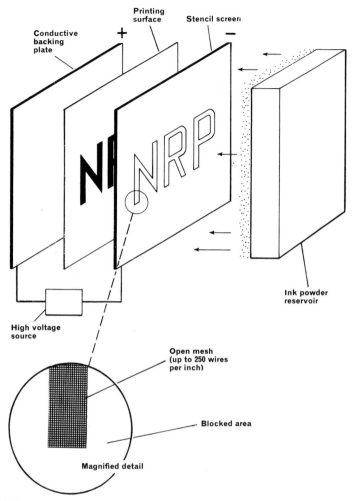

Conductive backing plate

Printing surface

Stencil screen

High voltage source

Ink powder reservoir

Open mesh (up to 250 wires per inch)

Blocked area

Magnified detail

A simplified diagram showing the principles of electrostatic printing, in which an image can be produced without contact between the printing surface and the image which is to be printed.

fixed by heat to form a permanent bond between powder and paper. This, in essence, is what happens in xerographic copying machines and, though the description makes it sound somewhat complicated, such machines can handle the copying of documents at quite high speeds. This is not, however, what we have learned to understand by the word 'printing': the copiers do not originate the images, and their functions are confined to the replication of those which already exist.

The use of a photo-electrically-produced charge nevertheless has considerable potential in printing. The 'exposure' of such a surface may be compared with the photographic exposure of plates such as those used in offset, and electrostatic offset plate production has been successfully used. The image on such plates is made visible by exposing the photo-electrically charged surface to 'ink', or rather to a fine powder similar to that used in the xerographic copying process and giving the printing areas the required characteristic for lithographic reproduction. The powder itself, in this case, consists of particles which are electrically charged in the opposite polarity to that of the surface, and the two, crudely speaking, stick together and are fixed by heat or solvent vapour.

It can be seen that, if paper is used, the electrostatic principle can be extended to the creating of printed images. Electrostatic principles have been used in screen process printing, where the powder is attracted to electrostatically-charged areas below the mesh of the screen. One significant difference between electrostatic printing and all other processes is that the stock to be printed does not need to come into direct contract with an image surface: the powder literally jumps the distance between the 'inking' unit and the stock. This has allowed electrostatic printing to be tried successfully on all sorts of otherwise unprintable surfaces, including the skins of soft fruits, such as peaches and avocado pears.

The present defects of electrostatic printing are in obtaining high speeds, comparable with the main processes, and in the need for powders in place of ductile inks, which present problems of keeping machinery and print clean over long runs. These are snags which seem reasonably susceptible of solution, and electrostatic printing certainly sug-gests some remarkable advantages over existing processes: different colour powders can be used and printed in a single pass of the paper through the machine, giving a multi-colour image instantaneously.

Looking yet further into the future, one can meditate on the feasibility of an electro-static charge being instantaneously induced in a pile of paper, so that the whole run, so to speak, is ready for printing and the paper needs only to be fed through an electrostatic printer to obtain the required number of replications. It is possible, too, to visualise the use of computers to output electrostatic 'signals' and, with the incorporation of the sophis-ticated systems of image origination and composition already described, to work directly to the 'presses' (electrostatic printing units, actually). Were this to become possible, we should, at last, see the final reduction of the gap between origination (pre-press) pro-cedures and printing which has exercised us so much in the preceding pages.

When contemplating these, and other, possibilities, which are on, or over, the horizons of today's commercial printers we should not forget that printing is an industry that cannot, by any stretch of the imagination, stand around waiting for 'the better mousetrap': it must cope, by all available means, with an existing and continuing demand, and do so within an existing structure of taste, style and, above all, cost. It is also relevant that printers are not themselves the final arbiters of the equipment available for their use. The machinery and materials manufacturers (and, to an increasing extent, the paper-makers and inkmakers) are faced with decisions and technical problems which are quali-tatively and quantitatively different from those we have discussed as belonging to the

Fluidics components design. Such components replace, by complex 'channelling' of fluids, the switching and other functions carried out by electronic means. Among the advantages of fluidic circuits is their comparatively high resistance to ambient conditions such as heat, humidity and vibration.

printing industry. The existence of a possible solution to a printing problem does not automatically produce the required equipment; costs of research are high and, ultimately, the production of new designs and improved methods must rest on the ability of manufacturers to recover their costs and make profits from sales. Printers have always shown themselves capable of ingenuity and inventiveness on their own behalf, and there can be few plants where some small item has not been designed and used further to extend the operational efficiency of a machine or to improve technique. The newer systems described under various headings in the preceding chapters are mostly capable of great flexibility and, by combination and adaptation, printers may now assemble equipment very closely suited to their particular needs or specialisations. It remains, however, a matter for sober judgement whether a printer can, or should, leap gratefully in the direction of each new development. In practice, few printers do so.

This is noticed (as I have already observed elsewhere) in the relative slowness with which photo-typesetting has gained ground. The hot-metal systems were built to last, and last they do. Heavy investment in conventional typesetting equipment, allied to the need for new skills and new procedures for progressing setting through the stages of origination, proofing, platemaking, etc, for photo-typesetting, have inhibited the apparently simple switch from metal to film which is theoretically desirable when photo-chemically based processes are used.

Any detailed consideration of the engineering, electronic and other development work which is going forward on behalf of the printer is outside my scope. I was, however, intrigued by the results of research recently conducted into the use of fluidic components in printing machinery. Whether the promises held out by modern fluidic technology in place of electro-mechanical and electronic controls are sound remains to be seen, and there is certainly little obvious enthusiasm for fluidics in present-day printing literature. I venture to predict that this will change, and that the new technology will eventually live up to the hopes which many have had of it.

Fluidics is a development of the earlier (and not always industrially successful) sciences of hydraulics and pneumatics. In place of the heavy shifting undertaken by mechanical systems based on the power of compressed air or fluid, modern fluidics uses a variety of components designed to use fluid pressures in ways more or less comparable to electrical, or electronic, flow. The fluidic components – switching devices mainly – are not, of course, so rapid in their responses as are electrically-powered systems, nor do they exhibit, as yet, the variety of uses to which advanced electronic controls are now put. They are, however, less susceptible to a machine environment which includes vibration, dirt and dust and changes in temperature. Fluidics circuits of advanced design will carry out storage and switching functions previously possible only with electronic circuits. A full discussion of fluidics would require a more detailed analysis of present and potential developments in this field than I propose to offer in a book of this kind; I mention fluidics here as yet another direction from which changes may come, particularly in press controls and in the sorting and batching operations common to the bindery and despatch departments of commercial printing plants and newspaper production plants.

It would be unwise to ignore a completely new range of possibilities which has arrived and which, for the first time in the history of printing, is exercising an influence by offering workable alternatives to the whole business of reproduction by printing methods: I refer to the various information storage and retrieval systems which enable images to be reduced to small size and kept as film. The retrieval of information stored in this way is now extremely rapid and efficient, and equipment exists which enables offset plates to be made from microfilmed originals for further replication by conventional printing. Methods are also available for the updating of microfilm files. While these methods cannot be compared with printing, in so far as they do not involve image origination in the sense in which the printer uses his various procedures of typesetting and illustration, they considerably further the uses to which simple origination via typewriters and other non-standard printing methods can be put. If information is accessible to those who need it from such microfilm 'banks' it is impossible not to predict a decline, in specific areas, for the more cumbersome and expensive products of the presses. A multi-access microfilm 'library' is, in a number of ways, as efficient as a library of printed material; it takes up less space, is capable of quicker updating and can be easier to use for specialised purposes.

Everything which has been said of microfilm storage can apply to computer storage of information, with added speed of access and extremely rapid and efficient means of introducing new or updated information. Many American universities and research centres are now using large central computers working to a number of terminals from which data can be extracted by methods no more complex, for the user, than the dialling of a telephone number. Indeed, one such set-up has replaced a printed telephone directory by a computer which stores numbers and provides terminal users with a display of a required number on request, together with information on new or changed numbers and other useful facilities.

A proportion of printing today, it must be admitted, is carried out in default of speedier methods of bringing information together in one place and making it available to those who may wish to use it. Expense cannot always be calculated in terms of production and materials costs, and it may be more important to have the right material available at the right time than to devise ways of printing it quickly. A computer utilisation called time-sharing has already enabled low-cost terminals to be leased with access to very large banks of computer storage by which users can 'tap in' to a variety of programs and obtain immediate response to requests for information kept up-to-date by the central computer. Here we are contemplating a development with immense potential, and one which could have an important bearing on future demand for print in certain large categories now served by the presses.

It is an over-simplification of the present complexity and diversity of communications to see such developments as those outlined above as 'competitors' of print. Information, by whatever means it is stored and reproduced, varies considerably in value. A telephone directory, for example, is highly valuable to those who wish to use the telephone system (as anybody who has tried to find a number in Moscow, where there is no directory, will confirm!). Its accuracy, also, is important, as is its availability to the many millions of people who need to use it. Here, then, is one item of print which must constantly find ways of improving itself. The most advanced and expensive methods of production and updating are not wasted if they mean that the directory will do its job better. For the same reasons it will be in this category of 'high-density' information that printing will be challenged by later systems of information storage and retrieval.

Scientific information may be equally, or more, vital to have in a readily accessible form by those who wish to use it, but here the numbers of people requiring that information may be quite small. In such immensely expensive projects as the American space programme computerised information storage is part of a much bigger expenditure and is necessary for many workers to keep pace with the changing information demands of the projects. Printing alone could not hope to serve such demands adequately. But in many

Fluidics technology is finding new applications in printing. Here an experimental fluidics rig is being developed at the Printing and Packaging Industries' Research Association for batching and sorting. Such equipment could have uses in the collating departments of printing plants, or in the despatch departments of newspaper and magazine production plants.

cases the multiplication of typeset or typewritten originals remains the most practicable way of storing and distributing information.

Durability is another factor in sustaining the status of the printed word. With a printed text we can take our own time to assimilate what it contains; we can refer forwards or back to check information and help our overall comprehension. The information is easily transportable: we can take a report with us on a train journey, or carry it home from the office or laboratory in a briefcase.

The sheer proliferation of information, and the multiplication of situations in which information needs to be assembled and correlated is a guarantee that the many different ways of recording, storing and reproducing it will continue to be necessary. Of these printing, as it has been described in this book, is still the most widely used, and still the one in most persistent demand. It is sometimes forgotten that modern systems of information storage and retrieval have, far from challenging printing on its own ground, created new categories of print: computers use printed material in many forms to carry out their tasks; business systems make demands on printing for a variety of documents, forms and other material which is consumed in large quantities daily.

I have tried to deal with some of the methods by which the printing industry has adjusted itself to change and to the varied demands of modern living as well as what has been retained and carried over from earlier times. I hope it has been shown that the printer's horizons have widened and that no single process or set of production techniques is adequate to every requirement. A postage stamp is still so different from a poster that it must be regarded as a different product, though both can be printed by the same process. Yet – and this is part of the magic which remains undimmed by the commerce of printing – every printed item we handle seems – and in a sense is – completely itself: completely unique. If you have bought this book it is 'yours'; a palpable thing; a possession, which has more individuality – more personality, if you will allow the use of the word – than the majority of factory-made objects with which we now surround ourselves. Most printers, though they may not show it, are deeply aware of this. In the more profound sense of creating good and useful things out of inks and paper, they are still craftsmen, though they may seek every possible way of reducing the amount of work which has to be done with hand and eye. The paradox exists, but matters less than the evidence which surrounds us of the continuing need for conscientiously made, skilled, finely judged and efficiently executed print.

Bibliography

Printing: the changing scene

Annals of Printing, W. T. Berry and H. E. Poole (Blandford, 1966)
The Penrose Annual, ed. Herbert Spencer (Lund Humphries)
The Printing Industry, Victor Strauss (Printing Industries of America and R. R. Bowker Co., 1967)
Methods of Book Design, Hugh Williamson (Oxford, 2nd ed., 1966)

Lithography: from stone to metal

Photolitho-Offset, Eric Chambers (Benn, 1967)

Letterpress: the first process

Modern Trends in Letterpress Printing, Peter Gibson (Studio Vista, 1966)
Letterpress Composition and Machinework, C. A. Hurst and F. R. Lawrence (Benn, 1963)
Printing by Letterpress, E. A. D. Hutchings (Heinemann, 1964)

Gravure: the giant

The Daily Telegraph Magazine Guide to Gravure, ed. Otto Lilien (Daily Telegraph, 1968)
Photogravure Process, G. C. Wensley (Benn, 1964)

Screen Process

Beginner's Book of Screen Process Printing, W. Clemence (Blandford, revised ed., 1970)
Silk Screen Process Production, H. K. Middleton (Blandford, 5th ed., 1967)

Composition: from keyboard to printed text

The Composition of Reading Matter, James Moran (Wace, 1965)
Photosetting, Andrew Bluhm (Pergamon, 1970)
Monotype Handbook (Monotype Corporation)
Linotype Handbook (Linotype & Machinery Ltd)

Typography and design

Typographic Design, Raymond Roberts (Benn, 1966)
Basic Typography, John R. Biggs (Faber, 1969)
An Introduction to Typography, Oliver Simon (Faber, 1963)
Printing Types (two volumes), D. B. Updike (Oxford, 3rd ed., 1962)
The Encyclopaedia of Type Faces, ed. W. T. Jaspert, W. T. Berry and A. F. Johnson
    (Blandford, 4th ed., 1970)
An Approach to Type, John Biggs (Blandford, revised ed., 1961)
Thoughts on Design, Paul Rand (Studio Vista, 2nd ed., 1970)

Illustration and reproduction

The Graphic Reproduction and Photography of Works of Art, John Lewis and Edwin
    Smith (W. S. Cowell, 1969)
The Illustration of Books, David Bland (Faber, 1969)
Ilford Graphic Arts Manual, vol. I: Photo-engraving, H. M. Cartwright (Ilford Ltd, 1962)
Graphic Design for the Computer Age E. A. Hamilton (Van Nostrand, 1970)

Computers in Print

Computer Peripherals and Typesetting, Arthur Phillips (H.M.S.O., 1968)

Bindery: finishing the job

The Making of Books, Sean Jennett (Faber, 4th ed., 1967)

Paper and Ink

The Nature of Paper and Board, F. H. Norris (Pitman, 1966)
Printing Ink Manual, ed. F. A. Askew (Heffer, 1963)

What happens next?

Computers, Office Machines and the New Information Technology, Carl Heyel (Macmil-
    lan, 1969)
'Information', a *Scientific American* book (Freeman, 1967)

Index